Poets of Devon & Cornwall

Shearsman Classics Vol. 1

Other titles in the *Shearsman Classics* series:

2. Robert Herrick: *Selected Poems*

Forthcoming in the same series:

3. *Spanish Poetry of the Golden Age,*
    in contemporary English translations (ed. Tony Frazer)
4. William Strode: *Selected Poems*
5. Sir Thomas Wyatt, *Selected Poems*
6. Mary, Lady Chudleigh: *Selected Poems*

Poets of Devon & Cornwall

from Barclay to Coleridge

Selected & edited by
Tony Frazer

Shearsman Books
Exeter

First published in the United Kingdom in 2007 by
Shearsman Books Ltd
58 Velwell Road
Exeter EX4 4LD

www.shearsman.com

ISBN-13 978-1-905700-50-9

ISBN-10 1-905700-50-4

Notes, selection, and editorial matter copyright © Shearsman Books Ltd, 2007.

The publisher gratefully acknowledges financial assistance from
Arts Council England.

Contents

Introduction	6
Alexander Barclay (1476-1522)	9
Humfrey Gifford (?1550-1589)	15
Richard Carew (1555-1620)	21
Sir Walter Ralegh (1555-1618)	27
Sir Arthur Gorges (?1557-1625)	39
George Peele (1558-1598?)	47
Anne Dowriche (1560-1613)	53
Joseph Hall (1574-1656)	59
John Ford (1586-1640)	65
William Browne (?1590-1645)	69
Robert Herrick (1591-1674)	77
William Strode (1602?-1645)	89
Sidney Godolphin (1610-1643)	101
Mary, Lady Chudleigh (1656-1710)	109
John Gay (1685-1732)	119
Samuel Taylor Coleridge (1772-1834)	125

Introduction

What room is there in the early 21st century for an anthology of the poets of Devon and Cornwall, where the youngest representative is Coleridge, who died almost 175 years ago? Well, this seemingly arbitrary selection – determined by place, and in which all but four of the authors were born in a sixty-year span – throws up a number of interesting figures who might not otherwise be quite so visible. It also reminds us of the major literary figures who have worked or been born in the two westernmost counties.

The selection begins and ends as it does for two simple reasons: I can find no significant poet prior to Alexander Barclay — although there have been interesting claims for the medieval *Gawain* poet having lived in Devon — and I wished to avoid the turgid work of the minor Victorian versifiers who seem to have been all too active in the latter part of the 19th century. When I began the selection, I was aware of the west-country origins, or connections, of the major names, but subsequently discovered the work of William Strode, Sir Arthur Gorges and Lady Chudleigh — all fine poets — not to mention John Ford and George Peele, whose Devon origins, and indeed whose non-dramatic verse had previously escaped me. Of the other poets offered here, some are of the very first rank, but all those included have something to offer the lover of poetry — these are not provincial makeweights, even if in some cases their works do not now fall quite as easily on the ear as they might have done in former times.

In the cases of Barclay and Richard Carew, the selections are actually translations, which may seem strange to the modern reader. In Barclay's case, the translations are decidedly free however, and *The Ship of Fools* features a number of verses interpolated by the translator, mentioning figures in the Ottery area. Carew's translation of Tasso, though incomplete, deserves to be better known than as a footnote to Fairfax's later version, and represents Carew's talents better than the occasional verses contained in his fascinating *Survey of Cornwall*.

The most famous figure included in the book is of course Sir Walter Ralegh, a figure almost of fable, given the extent of his exploits. His poetry was much esteemed in his day, at a time when all gentlemen courtiers seem to have been able to turn their hand to the composition of verse, but little of it was published and almost none of it with an incontrovertible attribution. Courtiers of the period usually shunned publication, alas — although we are indebted to Sir Arthur Gorges, Ralegh's cousin, for compiling a collection of his own poems and translations in manuscript. This leaves the modern editor with a puzzle over which of Ralegh's poems one might safely include: a recent compilation[1] of his poetry was organised on the basis of declining likelihood of authorship. The results are chastening, with only some 35 poems surviving the cull and not all of those being certainties. The quality of these poems is however very high indeed and gives the modern reader some idea of why Ralegh was held in such esteem by major writers such as Spenser and Sidney.

At the other end of the time-scale we have Coleridge, another giant: the selection here concentrates on early works composed in Devon or across the border in Somerset, or on poems with local themes. One great poem thus qualifies: 'Kubla Khan', composed while the poet lived on Exmoor.

Robert Herrick should need no introduction. He wrote the majority of his work in Devon, while Vicar of Dean Prior, and he is without doubt one of the great poets of the Caroline era. His contemporary, Sidney Godolphin, who was killed in a Civil War skirmish at Chagford on Dartmoor, is a poet who should be better known, although it is true that not all of his work is of the first rank. There is enough there, however, to make him worthy of our time and attention today.

I would have liked to have been able to include more women poets, but social conventions for most of the period covered here tended to prevent women from publishing their work — which leaves us with only two women, the sternly Protestant Anne Dowriche, and the robust proto-feminist Lady Chudleigh, whose work should be considered amongst the most significant of her era. Both women deserve inclusion on their own merits.

Of the remaining poets, William Strode is woefully under-rated. Whilst researching this selection I acquired the only collected edition of his poetry, published in 1907, and was surprised to find that the volume still had uncut pages — a sad fate for a poet whose best work is still worth reading today, and whose consignment to oblivion owes more perhaps to the stature of his contemporaries than to any deficiencies in his own work. Then there is William Browne, a significant figure in his day but one whose work is now unfashionable, given its Arcadian pastoral themes. Humfrey Gifford, about whom little is known, and Joseph Hall, Bishop of Exeter while Herrick was at Dean Prior, both offer additional evidence that Devon was hardly lacking in talent in the 16th and 17th centuries.

John Gay was probably the most successful of the poets here in his own time, in terms of sales and broader reputation. A populist, as befits the author of *The Beggar's Opera*, much of his other work does not survive the passage of time well, but a small selection such as that offered here gives a fascinating glimpse into the world of 18th century London.

The poems selected for this anthology have been lightly updated, modern spelling being applied except in cases where the scansion would be adversely affected, but period punctuation has been retained where I have been able to verify its accuracy.

The Shearsman Classics series — which is not devoted solely to regional writers — will include individual volumes dedicated to some of these poets, beginning with Herrick in 2007; books devoted to Chudleigh and Strode will follow in 2008.

Tony Frazer,
Exeter, 2007

---

[1] *The Poems of Sir Walter Ralegh. A Historical Edition.* Edited by Michael Rudick, Renaissance English Text Society, Tempe, Arizona, 1999.

Alexander Barclay

Alexander Barclay was born around 1476. His place of birth is disputed, but one source who seems to have known him said that was born "beyond the cold river of Twede", i.e. in Scotland. His early years were spent in Croydon, and at some point he took a degree. He was ordained in 1508.

Barclay was appointed chaplain of the college of Ottery St Mary in the first decade of the 1500s. There, in 1509, he wrote his satirical poem, *The Ship of Fools*, a free translation from Sebastian Brant's German poem *Das Narrenschiff* (1494), which was popular throughout Europe at that time, although Barclay seems to have based his version more on the Latin translation than on the German original. *The Ship of Fools* was as popular in Barclay's version as it had been in Germany, and it marked the beginning of a new satirical literature in English.

In 1513, Barclay seems to have become a monk in the Benedictine monastery of Ely. It was probably here that he wrote his *Eclogues* (translations from Italian), but in 1520 "Maistre Barkleye, the Blacke Monke and Poete" was requested to devise "histoires and convenient raisons to florisshe the buildings and banquet house withal" at the meeting between Henry VIII and François I at the Field of the Cloth of Gold.

It is presumed that he went along with the religious changes as, under Edward VI, he retained the livings of Great Baddow and of Wookey, and acquired the rectory of All Hallows, in London's Lombard Street, in 1552. Shortly after this last preferment, he died at Croydon, where he was buried.

The text offered here retains some old spellings where the scansion demands it, or where no modern version exists. Sometimes, every syllable in a word should be pronounced, as if the word were French: thus *occasion* is not o-KAY-zhun, but o-KA(Y)-zee-on, and *devotion* is dee-VO-see-on.

Further Reading:
Eclogues of Alexander Barclay, Priest (ed. Beatrice White, Early English Text Society, 1928; reprinted with corrections, 1961).
The Ship of Fools (Richard Pynson, London, 1513; John Cawood, London, 1570; William Paterson, Edinburgh, 1874).

from *The Ship of Fools*

Here begynneth the foles and first inprofytable bokes

I am like other clerks which so frowardly them guide.
That after they are honest come unto promotion
They give them to pleasure their study set aside.
Their avarice covering with feigned devotion.
Yet daily they preach: and have great derision
Against the rude laymen: and all for covetyse.
Though their own conscience be blinded with that vice.

But if I durst trouth plainly utter and express.
This is the special cause of this inconvenience.
That greatest fools, and fullest of lewdness
Havinge least wit: and simplest science
Are first promoted: and have greatest reverence
For if one can flatter, and bear a hawk on his fist
He shall be made Parson of Honiton or of Clyst.

But he that is in study ay firm and diligent.
And without all favour preacheth Christus lore
Of all the comontye nowadays is sore shent.
And by estates threatened to prison oft therefore.
Thus what avail is it, to us to study more:
To know other scripture, truth, wisdom, or virtue
Since few, or none without favour dare them shew.

But O noble Doctors, that worthy are of name:
Consider our old fathers: note well their diligence:
Ensue ye their steps: obtain ye such fame,
As they did living: and that by true prudence.
Within their hearts they planted their science
And not in pleasant books. But now too few such be.
Therefore in this ship let them come row with me.

[*frowardly*: perversely; *covetyse*: covet; *comontye*: community; *shent*: put to shame/disgraced; *ensue*: follow]

*Of leapings and dances and fools that pass
their time in such vanity.*

Those folys a place may challenge in my ship
Which void of wisdom as men out of their mind
Them self delight to dance to leap and skip
In compass running like to the world wide
In unkind labour, such folys pleasure find
Running about in this their furious vice
Like as it were in Bacchus' sacrifice

Or as the druydans runneth in vain about
In their mad feasts upon the hill of yde
Making their sacrifice with furore noise and shout
Whan their madness setteth their wit aside
Or when the priests of mars all night abide
Within their temple by use abominable
To their idolys doing their service detestable

Like as these paynyms hath to their idols done
Their sacrifice wand'ring in their madness
Their bodies wearying, in vain wasting their shone
So do these folys them self to dancing dress
Seeking occasion of great unhappiness
They take such labour without all hope of gain
Without reward sure, of wearyness and pain

Say folys that use this fury and outrage
What causeth you to have delight therein
For your great labour say what is your wage
Forsooth ye can thereby no profit win
But seek occasion (as I have said) of sin
And for thy wearing thy feet thus in the dust
Thou gettest no gain but cause of carnal lust

But when I consider of this foolish game
The first beginning and cause original
I say the cause thereof is worthy blame
For when the devil to deceive man mortal
And do contempt to the high god eternal
Upon a stage had set a calf of gold.
That every man the same might clear behold

So than the fend ground of misgovernance
Caused the people this figure to honour
As for their god and before the same to dance.
When they were drunken, thus fell they in error
Of idolatry, and forgot their creator.
Before this idol dancing both wife and man
Despising God: Thus dancing first began

Such blind folyes and inconvenience
Engendreth great hurt and incommodity
And seweth seed whereof groweth great offence
The ground of vice and of all enormity
In it is pride, foul lust and lechery
And while lewd leaps are usèd in the dance
Oft froward bargains are made by countenance

What else is dancing but even a nursery
Or else a bait to purchase and maintain
In young hearts the vile sin of ribaldry
Them fest'ring therein, as in a deadly chain
And to say truth in words clear and plain
Venereous people have all their whole pleasance
Their vice to nourish by this unthrifty dance

And wanton people disposèd unto sin
To satisfy their mad concupiscence
With hasty course unto this dancing ryn
To seek occasion of vile sin and offence

And to express my mind in short sentence
This vicious game oft times doth attyse
By his lewd signs, chaste heartis unto vice

Than it in earth no game is more damnable
It seemeth no peace, but battle openly
They that it use of minds seem unstable
As mad folk runnng with clamour shout and cry
What place is void of this furious folly
None: so that I doubt within a while
These folys the holy church shall defile

Of people what sort or order may we find
Rich or poor high or low of name
But by their foolishness, and wanton mind
Of each sort some are given unto the same
The priestis and clerks to dance have no shame
The frere or monk in his frock and cowl
Must dance in his dortor leaping to play the fool

To it cometh children, maids and wives.
And flattering young men to see to have their prey
The hand in hand great falsehood oft contrives
The old queen also this madness will assay
And the old dotard though he skantly may
For age and lameness steer other foot or hand
Yet playeth he the fool with other in the band

Than leap they about as folk past their mind
With madness amazèd running in compace
He most is commended that can most lewdness find
Or can most quickly run about the place
There are all manners usèd that lack grace
Moving their bodies in signs full of shame
Which doth their hearts to sin right sore inflame

So oft this vice doth many one abuse
That when they are departed from the dance
On lust and sin continually they muse
Having therein their will and their pleasance
Than fall they oft to great misgovernance
As folys given to work unprofitable
So in my ship they well deserve a babel.

* * *

[*druydans*: druids; *yde*: probably 'Ide,' as in Ides, a druidic festival day; *idolys*: idols; *paynyms*: pagans, heathens; *fend*: either fiend/fiendish, or defended; *froward*: perverse; *ryn*: run; *attyse*: entice; *heartis*: hearts; *folys*: fools; *priestis*: priests; *frere*: friar; *dortor*: dormitory; *compace*: compass;]

The Envoy of Barclay to The Fools

Ye obstinate folys that often fall in vice
How long shall ye keep this froward ignorance
Submit your minds, and so from sin arise
Let meekness slake your mad misgovernance
Remember that worldly pain it grievance
To be compared to hell which hath no peer
There is still pain, this is a short penance
Wherefore correct thy self while thou art here.

Humfrey Gifford

Humfrey Gifford (ca. 1550-1589), came from a well-to-do Devon family, and served as an official at the Poultry Counter, a debtors' prison. He was educated at Hart Hall, Oxford, and graduated in 1567. His sole publication was *A Posie of Gilloflowers, eche differing from other in colour and odour, yet all sweete.* (i.e. A Posy of Gillyflowers, each differing from [the] other in colour and odour, yet all sweet). *Imprinted at London for John Perin, and are to be solde at his shop in Paules Churchyard, at the signe of the Angell.* This was published in 1580. Little else is known of his life.

Collections of his work reappeared in the Victorian era, but he has been little anthologised in recent years.

Further Reading:
The Complete Poems and Translations in Prose of Humfrey Gifford, Gentleman (C.E. Simms, Manchester, 1875)
Humfrey Gifford: *A Posie of Gilloflowers, etc.* (Hawthornden Press, 1933)

In the praise of Friendship

Reveal (O tongue) the secrets of my thought,
Tell forth the game that perfect friendship brings:
Express what joys by her to man are brought,
Unfold her praise which glads all earthly things:
If one might say, in earth a heaven to be,
It is no doubt, where faithful friends agree.

To all estates true friendship is a stay,
To every wight a good and welcome guest:
Our life were death, were she once ta'en away,
Consuming cares would harbour in our breast.
Foul malice eke, would banish all delight,
And puff us up with poison of despight.

If that the seeds of ennui and debate,
Might yield no fruit, but wither and decay;
No cankered minds would hoard up heaps of hate.
No hollow hearts dissembling parts should play.
No clawback then would fawn in hope of mead,
Such life to lead, were perfect life indeed.

But nowadays desire of worldly pelfe,
With all estates makes friendship very cold:
Few for their friends, each shifteth for himself,
If in thy purse thou hast good store of gold:
Full many a one, thy friendship will embrace,
Thy wealth once spent, they turn away their face.

Let us still pray unto the Lord above,
For to relent our hearts as hard as stone:
That through the world one knot of loyal love,
In perfect truth might link us all in one:
Then should we pass this life without annoys,
And after death possess eternal joys.

New-Year's gift to Mistress C. P.

Sweet wight be glad, pluck up your sprites,
  Old friendship is renewed:
Mild concord hath thrown down the broth,
  That discord lately brewed.
Foul ennui, malice, and debate,
  In tears their time do spend:
In that the platform which they laid,
  Came not to wishèd end.
The mighty love, which ruleth all,
  Their prayers heard, no doubt:
Else could not their hot kindled wrath,
  So soon be quenched out.
Thus far their fury did prevail,
  A time and place was set,
Whereas at their appointed hour,
  To try it out, they met,
And dealt. For vows had rashly passed,
  So long foes to abide:
Until the one, the others force,
  In open field had tried:
I shrink, to think what horror great,
  Now gripes your heart through fear.
I seem to see each member quake,
  As if ye had been there:
To hear my muse unto your ears.
  This doleful tale to tell.
Put fear to flight, cast care aside,
  All things are ended well:
But rancour vile, couldst thou pow'r forth,
  Thy spite upon none other:
But that to combat thou must bring,
  My father and my brother?
And I myself with eyes must see,

And view this doleful sight?
Go pack, thou hast sustained the foil,
   For all thy poisoned might.
For by the blows that they did give,
   Their friendship doth increase,
And in their hearts established is,
   An everduring peace.
The seeds that thou in them didst plant,
   Are plucked up by the root:
Thy sister discord never shall,
   Again set in her foot.
For if in dealing of their blows,
   Their hands had not been blessed:
A late repent had made them rue,
   For harbouring such a guest.
But of ungrate discourtesies,
   We justly might complain:
In that entreaties would not serve,
   To make them friends again.
If in their mad and brainsick heads,
   Dame Reason had born sway:
But malice, rancour, and debate,
   Had banished wit away.
So that occasion of this broil,
   Was not our faithful friends:
But these forenamed furies fell,
   And other hellish fiends.
Whose daily drifts are to deface,
   Of friends the pure estate:
And makes them harbour in their hearts,
   Great heaps of deadly hate:
In that things past, betwixt them are
   Forgiven and forgot:
Let us embrace and love them so,
   As if this happened not.

If strange it seems, that stranger I,
   In verse to you do write:
Assure yourself, it doth proceed,
   Through greatness of delight,
That I conceive in that I see,
   Them reconciled so well,
Whom no persuasions lately served,
   Their furies to expel.
These simple verses to your view,
   I have thought good to send,
In token of a good new year,
   And so farewell, I end.

The complaint of a sinner

Like as the thief in prison cast,
   With woeful wailing moans,
When hope of pardon clean is past,
   And sighs with doleful groans:
So I a slave to sin,
   With sobs and many a tear,
As one without thine aid forlorn,
   Before thy throne appear.

O Lord, in rage of wanton youth
   My follies did abound,
And eke, since that I knew thy truth,
   My life hath been unsound.
Alas I do confess,
   I see the perfect way,
Yet frailty of my feeble flesh,
   Doth make me run astray.

Aye me, when that some good desire,
   Would move me to do well,
Affections fond make me retire,
   And cause me to rebel.
I wake, yet am asleep,
   I see, yet still am blind,
In ill I run with headlong race,
   In good I come behind.

Lo thus in life I daily die,
   And dying shall not live,
Unless thy mercy speedily,
   Some succour to me give.
I die O Lord, I die,
   If thou do me forsake,
I shall be likened unto those,
   That fall into the lake.

wight: person;
despight: spite; disregard;
pelfe: wealth; riches;
eke: moreover

Richard Carew

Richard Carew (pronounced Carey, 1555-1620), was of the long-established Carew family of Antony in Cornwall, and was born at Antony House. He went up to Christ Church College, Oxford, at the age of eleven, and at fourteen was selected to participate in a debate with Sir Philip Sidney in the presence of the Earls of Warwick and Leicester. There is, alas, no record of the subject of this debate. After Oxford he attended the Middle Temple for three years, and then travelled abroad. In 1584 he entered Parliament, and in 1586 was appointed High-Sheriff of Cornwall. He served as Treasurer under Sir Walter Ralegh during the latter's term as Lord Lieutenant of the county. He married Juliana Arundel in 1597.

Carew became a member of the Society of Antiquaries in 1589, and his major publication in this connection is the fascinating *A Survey of Cornwall* (1602). His other writings include *Epistle concerning the Excellencies of the English Tongue* (1605). As a translator he is today best remembered for his version of the first five cantos of *Gerusalemme Liberata* (Jerusalem Delivered, 1580) by Torquato Tasso (1544-1595), an Italian heroic epic poem concerning Godefroi de Bouillon, leader of the First Crusade, of which a part is presented here. It was published under the title *Godfrey of Balloigne, or the Recouerie of Hierusalam; The Examination of Men's Wits* in 1594. He also translated a minor treatise by John Huarte, *Examen de Ingenios*, although his version is from an Italian translation rather than the Spanish original.

Richard Carew is related to the later Cavalier poet Thomas Carew, but his kinsman was born in Kent and seems to have had no connection with the West Country, other than his blood ties.

Further Reading:
Richard Carew: *The Survey of Cornwall, 1602*. (Bossiney Books, Launceston, 2004) – unabridged edition, with modernised spelling.

from Jerusalem: The First Song

I sing the godly arms, and that chieftain,
Who great sepulchre of our Lord did free,
Much with his hand, much wrought he with his brain,
Much in his glorious conquest suffered he,
And hell in vain itself opposed, in vain
The mixed troops Asian and Libick flee
To arms, for heaven him favoured, and he drew
To sacred ensigns his strayed mates anew.

O Muse, thou that they head not compassest
With fading bays, which Helicon doth bear,
But 'bove in skies, amidst the choirs blessed,
Dost golden crown of stars immortal wear,
Celestial flames breath thou into my breast,
Enlighten thou my song, and pardon where
I fainings weave with truth, and verse with art,
Of pleasings decked, wherein thou hast no part.

Thou knowst, where luring Parnass most pours out
His sweetness, all the world doth after run,
And that truth seasoned with smooth verse, from doubt
The waywardst (flocking) to believe hath won,
So cup, his brims erst liquoriced about
With sweet, we give to our diseased son.
Beguiled he drinks some bitter juice the while,
And doth his life receive from such a guile.

Thou noble minded Alphonse, who doest save
From fortune's fury, and to port dost steer
Me wand'ring pilgrim, midst of many a wave,
And many a rock betossed, and drenched well near,
My verse with friendly grace t' accept vouchsafe,
Which as in vow, sacred to thee I bear.

One day perhaps, my pen forehastening
Will dare what now of thee tis purposing.

If ever Christians to agreement grow,
And with their navy and their force by land,
A pray so great and wrong from Turkish foe
Seek to regain, due reason doth command
That of that soil the sceptre they bestow,
Or of those seas, if so thy pleasure stand,
On thee, thou Godfrey's countermate, my rhyme
Attend, and arms provide in this mean time.

Since Christian camp for high exploit to th' East
Had passed, the last of six years on now ran,
And Nice by force, and Antioch not least
Of power, by warlike policy they wan.
Wheregainst when Persians passing number pressed,
In battle bold they it defended than.
And Tortose gat, which done, to winter's reign
They yield, and stay the coming year again.

The season, by his kind inclined to weat,
Which lays up arms, weary his course now ends,
When Sire eternal from his lofty seat,
Which in the purest part of heaven extends,
And from the lowest hell, what space is great
To stars, so far above the stars ascends,
Looks down, and in one blink, and in one view,
Compriseth all what so the world can shew.

Each thing he views, and then he set his eye
On Syria, where Christian princes stay,
And with that sight, which piercingly can spy
What closet up humane affections lay,
He Godfrey sees, who panims lewd to fly

From sacred city would enforce away.
And full of faith, and full of zeal in heart,
All worldly wealthy, rule, glory, lays apart.

But he in Baldwin sees a greedy vain,
Which bent to human greatness high aspires,
He Tancred sees, his life hold in disdain,
So much a fond love him afflicting fires,
And Bohemond he sees, for his new reign
Of Antioch foundations deep desires
To ground, and laws enacts, and orders lathe
And arts brings in, and plants the Christian faith.

And in this course he entered is so far,
That ought but that it seems of nought he ways,
He scries Rinaldo's mind, addict to war,
And working spirits, much abhorring ease,
No lust of gold in him, no thoughts there are
Of rule, but great and much enflamed of praise,
He scries that at the mouth he hangs of Guelph,
And old examples rare frames to himself.

When inmost sense of these and other sprights
The King of all the world had full unfold,
He calls him to, of the angelic lights
Him that 'mongst first the second rank doth hold.
A faithful truchman, Gabriel that hights,
A nuncio glad, twixt souls of better mould,
And God to us down heaven's decrees who shows,
And up to heav'n who with men's prayers goes.

God to his nuncio said, "Seek Godfrey out,
And tell him in my name, why stands he still?
The wars again who goes he not about?
Jerusalem oppressed to free from ill,

Captains to counsel let him call, and rout
Of sluggards raise, that he be chief I will.
There him choose, and those below that are
Tofore his mates, shall be his men of war."

So spake he, Gabriel himself addressed,
Swift to perform the things in charge he takes.
His shape unseen, with air he doth invest,
And unto mortal sense his subject makes,
Man's limbs, man's look, t' appearence he possessed,
Which yet celestial majesty pertakes:
Twixt youth and childhood bounded seem his days,
His golden locks he doth adorn with rays.

He puts on silver wings, yfringed with gold,
Weariless nimble, of most pliant sway,
With these he parts the winds and clouds, and hold
Doth flight with these aloft the earth and sea.
Attired thus, to the world's lower mould
This messenger of skies directs his way;
On Liban mountain hov'ring first he stayed,
And twixt his eagle wings himself he weighed.

Therehence again to pastures of Tortose,
Plump down directly levels he his flight.
From eastern coast the new sun then arose,
Part up, but of more part waves hid the sight,
And early Godfrey that mornetide bestows
In prayer to God, as aye his usage night.
When like the sun, but far and far more clear
Th' angel to him doth from th' east appear.

And thus bespake Godfrey: "Now season tides,
That best with warrior's service doth agree.
Why thwart you ling'ring then, while fast it slides,

And not Jerusalem from thraldom free?
Do thou to council call the people's guides,
Do thou the slow their work to finish see.
God for their chieftain thee hath deemed fit,
And glad at once they shall themselves submit.

"God me this message sent, and I reveal
To thee his mind in his own name, how great
A hope of victory to have? A zeal
How great, of host thy charge hooves thee to heat?"
He ceased, and vanished flew to th' upper deal,
And purest portion of the heavenly seat.
Godfrey those words, and that his shining bright
Dazzled in eyes, and did in heart affright.

But fright once gone, and having well bethought,
Who came, who sent, and what to him was said,
Of erst he wished, he now a fire hath caught
To end the war whose charge God on him laid.
Not for the heav'ns him sole this honour brought,
Ambitious wind puffing his stomach swayed,
But all his will did more in will enflame
Of his dear Lord, as spark becomes a flame.

Then his heroic mates dispersed about,
But not far off, t'assemble he invites:
Letter to letter, message on message out
He sends, advice with prayer he unites
What so may flock or prick a courage stout,
What skill dull virtue to awake endites:
Seems all he finds, with efficacy such
As he enforceth, yet contenteth much.

[*truchman*: interpreter; *panim*: pagan; *guelph*: member of a pro-papal faction in Italy, opposed to the Holy Roman Emperor; *nuncio*: diplo-mat, representative; *hights*: is called; *Liban*: Lebanon; *endites*: indicts]

Sir Walter Ralegh

Walter Ralegh (sometimes incorrectly spelled Raleigh, and pronounced *Rawley*) was born into a gentleman's family at Hayes Barton, near Budleigh Salterton, Devon, ca. 1555. He studied at Oriel College, Oxford, fought on the Huguenot side in the French Wars of Religion, and subsequently attended the Middle Temple, although whether this was as a law student or not is unclear: the Inns acted in this period as a kind of training-ground for young men seeking preferment at Court, and not only as a law school.

Early in his career he sailed to the Azores and the West Indies under Sir Humphrey Gilbert, and then made a name for himself with the army in Ireland. His success there, and no doubt his striking looks – he was about six feet tall, handsome, and as well-dressed as any man of his time – brought him to the attention of Queen Elizabeth I, and his rapid ascent began. During the 1580s he acquired monopolies that increased his income considerably, as well as large estates in occupied Ireland; he was made Captain of the Queen's Guard, and was given the use of Durham House in the Strand. He became MP for Devon in 1584 and sat in Parliament for the next two years. In 1585 he was knighted, became the Warden of the Stannaries (i.e. in charge of the Cornish tin-mines), and Lord Lieutenant of Cornwall. In 1592 he purchased Sherborne Manor in Dorset as a family home.

He had married Elizabeth Throckmorton, one of the Queen's ladies-in-waiting, in the late 1580s, but had kept this a secret from the Queen, only to be discovered when his wife gave birth to her first child. The Queen appears to have been jealous, and had both Ralegh and his wife locked up in the Tower of London. Ralegh managed to buy his way out of the Tower with the profits from a voyage in which he had invested, but never regained his privileged position at court.

In 1585, he had sponsored the first English colony in America near Roanoke Island, in what is today North Carolina, a colony that he named Virginia for his Queen. This colony failed however, and a further attempt at colonisation also failed in 1587. In 1595 he led a further expedition to the Orinoco River in Guiana (modern Venezuela), and described his experiences in a book, *The*

Discoverie of Guiana, published in 1596. It was on this voyage that the rumours of fabled El Dorado reached him, and although he wished to establish a colony in Guiana, there was little support. He was to undertake further expeditions, including an attempted raid on Cádiz.

With the accession of James I to the throne in 1603, and a more careful official policy towards Spain, Ralegh rapidly fell from favour, partly due to plotting by his enemies at Court. He was accused of plotting against the King and was sentenced to death in 1603, only to have his sentence commuted to life imprisonment. During his incarceration he wrote *The Historie of the Worlde* (1614), a remarkable display of scholarship. He managed to arrange his release, but not a pardon, in 1616, in order to finance and lead a new expedition to the coast of Guiana, partly to found a new goldmine, but with instructions not to upset Spain in the process. This journey resulted in total failure, the destruction of a Spanish settlement, and the acquisition of no gold. Upon Ralegh's ignominious return, the King revoked his suspended sentence, and he was re-incarcerated and executed two years later. He has been a romantic figure of English history ever since, although his personal achievements were outstripped by his literary achievements – even if today we are able to identify securely only some thirty poems. In his own time, and for some years after his death, Ralegh was counted amongst the very greatest poets of the age.

Further reading:
The Poems of Sir Walter Ralegh. A Historical Edition. Edited by Michael Rudick, Renaissance English Text Society, Tempe, Arizona, 1999.
The Letters of Sir Walter Ralegh, ed. Latham & Youings, Exeter University Press, Exeter, 1999.
Selected Writings ed. Gerald Hammond, Penguin Books, Harmondsworth, 1984.
The Discoverie of the Large, Rich and Bewtiful Empyre of Guiana, Manchester University Press, Manchester, 1997.

A Vision Upon This Conceit of The Fairie Queen

Methought I saw the grave, where Laura lay,
Within that temple, where the vestal flame
Was wont to burn, and passing by that way,
To see that buried dust of living fame,
Whose tomb fair love, and fairer virtue kept,
All suddenly I saw the Faery Queen:
At whose approach the soul of Petrarch wept,
And from thenceforth those graces were not seen.
For they this Queen attended, in whose steed
Oblivion laid him down on Laura's hearse.
Hereat the hardest stones were seen to bleed,
And groans of buried ghosts the heavens did pierce:
    Where Homer's sprite did tremble all for grief,
    And cursed th' access of that celestial thief.

As you came from the holy land

As you came from the holy land
  of Walsingham—
Met you not with my true love
  by the way as you came—
How shall I know your true love
That have met many one
As I went to the holy land
That have come that have gone
She is neither white nor brown
But as the heavens fair
There is none hath a form so divine
In the earth or the air
Such a one did I meet good sir
Such an angelic face

Who like a queen like a nymph did appear
by her gait by her grace:
She hath left me here all alone,
All alone as unknown
Who sometimes did me lead with her self,
And me loved as her own:–
What's the cause that she leaves you alone,
And a new way doth take:
Who loved you once as her own
And her joy did you make:
I have loved her all my youth
But now old as you see
Love likes not the falling fruit
From the withered tree:
Know that love is a careless child
And forgets promise past:
He is blind, he is deaf when he list,
And in faith never fast:
His desire is a dureless content
And a trustless joy
He is won with a world of despair
And is lost with a toy:
Of womankind such indeed is the love
Or the word Love abused
Under which many childish desires
And conceits are excused.
But true Love is a durable fire
In the mind ever burning:
Never sick never old never dead,
From itself never turning.

An Epitaph upon the right Honourable
Sir Philip Sidney, Knight, Lord Governor of Flushing

To praise thy life, or wail thy worthy death,
And want thy wit, thy wit high, pure, divine,
Is far beyond the pow'r of mortal line,
Nor any one hath worth that draweth breath.

Yet rich in zeal, though poor in learning's lore,
And friendly care obscured in secret breast,
And love that envy in thy life suppressed,
That dear life done, and death hath doubled more.

And I, that in thy time and living state,
Did only praise thy virtues in my thought,
As one that seeld the rising sun hath sought,
With words and tears now wail thy timeless fate.

Drawn was thy race aright from princely line,
Nor less than such, (by gifts that nature gave,
The common mother that all creatures have,)
Doth virtue show, and princely lineage shine.

A king gave thee thy name, a kingly mind,
Which God thee gave, who found it now too dear
For this base world, and hath resumed it near,
To sit in skies, and sort with pow'rs divine.

Kent thy birthdays, and Oxford held thy youth,
The heavens made haste, and stayed nor years, nor time,
The fruits of age grew ripe in thy first prime,
Thy will, thy words; thy words, the seals of truth.

Great gifts and wisdom rare employed thee thence,
To treat from kings, with those more great than kings,

Such hope men had to lay the highest things,
On thy wise youth, to be transported hence.

Whence to sharp wars sweet honour did thee call,
Thy country's love, religion, and thy friends:
Of worthy men, the marks, the lives and ends,
And her defence, for whom we labour all.

There didst thou conquer shame and tedious age,
Grief, sorrow, sickness, and base fortune's might;
Thy rising day, saw never woeful night,
But passed with praise, from off this worldly stage.

Back to the camp, by thee that day was brought,
First thine own death, and after thy long fame;
Tears to the soldiers, the proud Castilian's shame;
Virtue expressed, and honour truly taught.

What hath he lost, that such great grace hath won,
Young years, for endless years, and hope unsure,
Of fortune's gifts, for wealth that still shall dure,
O happy race with so great praises run.

England doth hold thy limbs that bred the same,
Flanders thy valour where it last was tried,
The camp thy sorrow where thy body died,
Thy friends, thy want; the world, thy virtue's fame;

Nations thy wit, our minds lay up thy love,
Letters thy learning, thy loss years long to come,
In worthy hearts sorrow hath built thy tomb,
Thy soul and spright enrich the heavens above.

Thy liberal heart embalmed in grateful tears,
Young sighs, sweet sighs, sage sighs, bewail thy fall,

Envy her sting, and spite hath left her gall,
Malice herself, a mourning garment wears.

That day their Hannibal died, our Scipio fell,
Scipio, Cicero, and Petrarch of our time;
Whose virtues, wounded by my worthless rhyme,
Let angels speak, and heaven thy praises tell.

[*spright*: spirit; *seeld*: blinded (a term from falconry)]

A Poesy to prove affection is not love

Conceit begotten by the eyes,
Is quickly born, and quickly dies:
For while it seeks our hearts to have,
Meanwhile there reason makes his grave:
For many things the eyes approve,
Which yet the heart doth seldom love.

For as the seeds in springtime sown,
Die in the ground ere they be grown,
Such is conceit, whose rooting fails,
As child that in the cradle quails,
Or else within the Mother's womb,
Hath his beginning, and his tomb.

Affection follows fortune's wheels;
And soon is shaken from her heels;
For following beauty or estate,
Her liking still is turned to hate.
For all affections have their change,
And fancy only loves to range.

Desire himself runs out of breath,
And getting, doth but gain his death:
Desire, nor reason hath, nor rest,
And blind doth seldom choose the best,
Desire attained is not desire,
But as the cinders of the fire.

As ships in ports desired are drowned,
As fruit once ripe, then falls to ground,
As flies that seek for flames, are brought
To cinders by the flames they sought:
So fond desire when it attains,
The life expires, the woe remains.

And yet some poets fain would prove,
Affection to be perfect love,
And that desire is of that kind,
No less a passion of the mind.
As if wild beasts and men did seek,
To like, to love, to choose alike.

Calling to mind

Calling to mind, mine eye went long about
    To cause my heart for to forsake my breast,
All in a rage, I thought to pluck it out,
    By whose device, I lived in such unrest.
What could it say then to regain my grace,
    Forsooth, that it had seen my mistress' face.

Another time I called unto mind,
    It was my heart, which all this woe had wrought

Because that he to love, his fort resigned,
    When on such wars, my fancy never thought.
What could he say, when I would have him slain
    That he was yours, and had forgone me clean.

At length when I perceived both eye and heart,
    Excuse themselves, as guiltless of my ill,
I found myself the cause of all my smart,
    And told myself, myself now slay I will.
Yet when I saw my self to you was true,
    I loved myself, because my self loved you.

Farewell false love

Farewell false love, thou oracle of lies,
    A mortal foe, an enemy to rest,
An envious boy, from whence all cares arise,
    A bastard born, a beast with rage possessed.
A way of error, a temple full of treason,
    In all effects, contrary unto reason.
A poisoned serpent, covered all with flow'rs,
    Mother of sighs, and murderer of repose.
A sea of sorrows, whence are drawn such show'rs,
    As moisture lends to every grief that grows.
A pool of guile, a nest of deep deceit
    A gilded hook, that holds a poisoned bait.
A fortress foiled, which reason did defend,
    A siren's song, a fever of the mind
A maze wherein affection finds no end,
    A raging cloud, that roves before the wind
A substance like the shadow of the sun
    A goal of grief, for which the wisest run.
A quenchless fire, a nurse of trembling fear,

A path that leads to peril and mishap,
A true retrait of sorrow and despair,
   An idle boy, that sleeps in pleasure's lap,
A deep mistrust of that which certain seems,
   And hope of that, which reason doubtful deems.
Since then thy trains, my younger years betray,
   And for my faith, ingratitude I find,
And sith repentance, doth thy wrongs bewray
   Whose course I see, repugnant unto kind,
False love, desire, and beauty frail, adieu,
   Dead is the rote, from whence such fancies grew.

[*retrait*: portrait; *bewray*: reveal]

Lady farewell

Lady farewell whom I in silence serve
   Would God thou knew'st the depth of my desire,
Then might I hope, though nought I can deserve,
   Some drop of grace, would quench my scorching fire.
But as to love unknown I have decreed,
   So spare to speak doth often spare to speed.

Yet better 'twere that I in woe should waste
   Than sue for grace and pity in despight
And though I see in thee such pleasures placed
   That feeds my joy and breeds my chief delight,
Withal I see a chaste consent disdain
   Their suits, which seek to win thy will again.

Then farewell hope, a help to each man's harm
   The wind of woe, hath torn my tree of trust,
Care quenched the coals, which did my fancy warm,

And all my help lies buried in the dust.
But yet amongst those cares which cross my rest,
This comfort grows, I think I love thee best.

[*despight*: disdain, scorn]

The Advice

Many desire, but few or none deserve
To win the fort of thy most constant will:
Therefore take heed, let fancy never swerve
But unto him that will defend thee still.
    For this be sure, the fort of fame once won,
    Farewell the rest, thy happy days are done.

Many desire, but few or none deserve
To pluck the flowers and let the leaves to fall;
Therefore take heed, let fancy never swerve,
But unto him that will take leaves and all.
    For this be sure, the flower once plucked away,
    Farewell the rest, thy happy days decay.

Many desire, but few or none deserve
To cut the corn, not subject to the sickle.
Therefore take heed, let fancy never swerve,
But constant stand, for mowers' minds are fickle.
    For this be sure, the crop being once obtained,
    Farewell the rest, the soil will be disdained.

Fortune hath taken away my love

Fortune hath taken away my love
My life's joy and my soul's heaven above
Fortune hath taken thee away my princess
My world's delight and my true fancy's mistress

Fortune hath taken thee away from me
Fortune hath taken all by taking thee
Dead to all joys I only live to owe
So now fortune become my fancy's foe

In vain my eyes in vain you waste your tears
In vain my sighs the smoke of mighty fears
In vain you search the earth and heavens above
In vain you search for fortune keeps my love

Then will I leave my love in fortune's hands
Then will I leave my love in worthless bands
And only love the sorrow due to me
Sorrow henceforth that shall my princess be

And only joy that fortune conquering kings
Fortune that rules on earth and earthly things
Hath ta'en my love in spite of virtue's might
So blind a goddess did never virtue right

With wisdom's eyes had but blind fortune seen
Then had my love my love for ever been
But love farewell though fortune conquer thee
No fortune base shall ever alter me.

Sir Arthur Gorges

Sir Arthur Gorges was born in 1557, most probably at the family manor house in Butshead, outside Plymouth, although claims have been made for his birth in Dorset. He was cousin to Sir Walter Ralegh and, like Ralegh, was one of the gentleman-volunteers to battle against the Spanish Armada. In 1597 he commanded the *War-Spite*, the ship in which Raleigh sailed as Vice Admiral under Robert Devereux, Earl of Essex, on the Islands voyage. Gorges was knighted in 1597. His first wife Douglas Howard, whom he married in 1584, was a great beauty, and was the subject of a famous poem by Edmund Spenser upon her early death. Gorges remarried in 1597.

In 1611, with Sir Walter Cope, he was one of the founders of a central office for the transaction and registration of the sale of land, tenements, and goods, and also mercantile and other businesses, called 'The Publicke Register for Generall Commerce'. He was MP for five different constituencies between 1584 and 1601.

His own poems have sometimes been confused with those of Ralegh, and his poem 'The gentle season of the year...' – in fact partly a translation from the French – had at times been ascribed to Sir Philip Sidney, but matters became much clearer in 1940 when his collected poems, *Vannetyes and Toyes of Yowth*, were discovered in manuscript. Two of the poems were in the author's own hand, and many of the others bore his autograph emendations. Gorges was also a translator, producing a version of Lucan's *Pharsalia*, and several versions of French poems, which are scattered throughout his *Vannetyes*. He died in 1625.

Further reading:
The Poems of Sir Arthur Gorges (ed. Helen Estabrook Sandison, Oxford University Press, London, 1953)
Raymond Gorges: *The Story of a Family Through Eleven Centuries* (privately printed, Boston, 1944)

The gentle season of the year

The gentle season of the year
hath made the blooming branch appear
and beautified the lands with flowers
The air doth savour with delight
the heavens do smile to see the sight
and yet mine eyes augment their showers

The meadows mantled all with green
the trembling leaves have clothed the treen
the birds with feathers new do sing
But I poor soul whom wrong doth wrack
attire myself in mourning black
whose leaf doth fall amidst his spring

And as we see the scarlet rose
in this sweet prime his bud disclose
whose hue is with the sun revived
So in this April of mine age
my lively colour doth assuage
because my sunshine is deprived

My heart that wanted was of yore
light as the wind to range and sore
in every place where beauty springs
Now only hovers over you
even as a bird that's taken new
and flutters but with clippèd wings

When all men else are bent to sport
then pensive I alone resort
into some solitary walk
As doth the doleful turtledove
who having lost her faithful love
sits mourning on some withered stalk

There to myself do I recount
how far my woes my joys surmount
how love requiteth me with hate
how all my pleasures end in pain
how happ doth show my hope but vain
how fortune frowns upon my state

And in this mood charged with despair
with vapoured sighs I dim the air
and to the gods make this request
That by the ending of my life
I may have truce with this strange strife
and bring my soul to better rest.

[*treen*: trees]

She that holds me under the laws of love

She that holds me under the laws of love
    on whom my mournful verse so oft complains
For those strange griefs that I through wrong do prove
    she is the court wherein my life remains
She is my prince of whom I would deserve
    and she alone to me can favour lend
She hath for courtiers thousands that do serve
    and only on her eyes for looks attend
Unto her love we would as fain aspire
    as others would in Court to honours rise
And as disgrace makes courtiers to retire
    so do her frowns cause malcontents likewise
Like to the court she is unconstant and unkind
    But from the court differs in this alone
That in the court men hope reward to find
    But following her such hope remaineth none

From your fair eyes the kindling sparks were sent

From your fair eyes the kindling sparks were sent
that first did set my fancy on a fire
before which time I knew not what it meant
to burn in love and languish in desire
But daily now as in your face I see
those graces grow, that makes you more to shine
so daily doth new flames arise in me
and more and more, consume this breast of mine
Now are they grown so far into extremes
that greater rage, with life I may not taste
then do you not increase, in beauty's beams
Except you would my limbs to cinders waste
Yet better 'twere, that I should perish so
than you to lose such praise and glory due
although a mean to help all this I know
if love with beauty might increase in you
Which if it fail, then love thou wantst device
that canst not make her subject to thy bow
whose gentle heart was never framed of ice
although her breast resemble driven snow.

Since course of kind ordains it to be so

Since course of kind ordains it to be so
that strongest steel should yield unto the flame
and every metal that in mine doth grow
doth want the power for to resist the same
Then do not blame this human heart of mine
To yield unto the force of flames divine.

And since likewise by proof and daily view
we find the fire to have such secret power
to try the gold were it be false or true
and basest dross from finest silver scour
Then be assured true is this heart of mine
That so is tried in flames that are divine.

But therewithall sweet friend you must presume
that as the fire can metals melt and try
So will the force thereof each thing consume
that therein doth too long a season lie
Then save with speed the heart more yours than mine
Which else consumes amidst these flames divine.

My heart I have oftimes bid thee beware

My heart I have oftimes bid thee beware
how thou becamst subject to cruel love
But of my words thou never tookest care
alluring hope, thy fancy so did move
Wherefore my heart, the harm remains to me
but thine the blame, if I a captive be.

Why say you so what fault was it of mine
to yield when I did find my self betrayed
Nay rather blame those spialls false of thine
that led me on where beauty ambush laid
Those eyes I mean that bribèd were so oft
with smiling looks sent from a murdering thought

And call to count the trumpet of thy mind
who did so friendly sound unto thy foes
That tongue of thine who trait'rously inclined

in parley did thy secrets all disclose
And thy right hand (who if the truth were known)
did oft subscribe, more yours than mine own

Why then my heart this last farewell receive
and ye false limbs that be betrayèd so
Alas sweet life as yet do not us leave
for though perchance may'st find a friendly foe
Who of her grace to thee may freedom give
in hope thereof I am content to live.

[*spialls*: spies]

Retire from me you pensive thoughts awhile

Retire from me you pensive thoughts awhile
decayers of my youth my strength and lively blood
And let sweet sleep my troubled head beguile
whilst you go bathe yourselves in Lethe's flood
Or if not so, till I have taken rest
my thoughts go lodge within my mistress' breast

Make known to her my wounds as yet but green
disclose the sparks not grown to be a flame
Which time itself will make too plainly seen
except I cloak these griefs of mine with game
A ready way to fly not find relief
for who will rue on him that hides his grief

Therefore my thoughts perform this last request
of my true heart a thrall become to love
that she may know from whence comes my unrest
as well as I her beauty's force do prove

Then will I hope this happy end to see
pity in her, and joy to reign in me

Until which time I vow to roam about
in deserted woods till life with love be spent
Where none but love shall know to find me out
nor love himself, but from my mistress sent
For whose sweet sake to show on me her power
my weal for woe, my sweet I change for sour

And more then that for though through her disdain
She chance to clip the wings off my desire
And of my hope throw out the latter main
and force with shame my fancies to retire
Yet shall my love not end with loss of breath
for thou my soul shalt serve her after death

The unripe fruits of wanton youth's desire

The unripe fruits of wanton youth's desire
    so diff'rent are to use from that they seem
As when we do unto their height aspire
    then most we loathe that we most dear did deem
To find ourselves so blinded in conceit
    instead of food to fawn on flatt'ring bait

To hunters' sports these joys compared may be
    who with delight, so long in chase do run
As that their game before their face do fly
    but lose their sport when they their prey have won
Then reason would that we should toys neglect
    as are but shows and nothing in effect

Whose small abode doth yield no more content
    then lickerish meats, that do the palate please
Whose pleasure fades, when as their taste is spent
    and only serve to nourish one disease
Whose count well made, low grief is all the gain
    where fading joys are bought with lasting pain

Yet well I wote that when these lines of mine
    shall come before my mistress' carping eyes
She will me taunt and say the fox is fine
    that loves no grapes because they hang too high
And seem to make that dainty to be found
    which all men see grow rife, upon the ground

[*lickerish*: tasty)

Sonnet

When at your hands of love the sugared fruit
    I did request in guerdon of my truth
You did allege to hinder such my suit
    good fame which did surpass delights of youth
But as a man I pleasure did prefer
    with those sweet joys which I in love do find
Before those dreams that make us think we err
    and live in awe of words that are but wind
For frankly speak and then sweet friend tell me
    in these great terms of fame what proof is found
That doth delight or with our sense agree
    on old wives' tales, a fancy vain you ground
For in conceit alone doth fame consist
    But pleasure you may taste of if you list.

[*guerdon*: reward, recompense; *list*: wish/desire]

George Peele

George Peele (1558-c.1598) came from a landed Devon family, but his birthplace is unknown. He was educated at Christ's Hospital, where his father was Clerk, and entered Pembroke College, Oxford, in 1571. In 1574 he went on to Christ Church, taking his B.A. in 1577, and M.A. in 1579. He went to London about 1580, and married a woman of property in 1583, whose wealth he quickly squandered. His reckless life was to become a byword for poor behaviour, which was emphasised by the use of his name in connection with the apocryphal *Merrie conceited Jests of George Peele* (printed in 1607). Many of the stories had done service before, but there are personal touches that are thought to be biographical.

As a writer Peele was best known for his dramatic works: his pastoral comedy *The Araignment of Paris*, presented before Queen Elizabeth in 1581, was printed anonymously in 1584. Other significant works were the *Famous Chronicle of King Edward the First, surnamed Edward Longshanks*; *Llewellyn, Rebel in Wales*; *The Battle of Alcazar*; *The Sinking of Queen Elinor*; *The Old Wives' Tale* and *The Love of King David and Fair Bathsheba*. Peele is also claimed to have contributed to the writing of Shakespeare's tragedy *Titus Andronicus*.

His occasional poems include 'The Honour of the Garter', which has a prologue containing Peele's judgments on his contemporaries, and 'Polyhymnia' (1590), a blank verse description of the ceremonies attending the retirement of the Queen's champion, Sir Henry Lee. One of his poems, 'The Praise of Chastity' features in the *Phoenix Nest* anthology (1593).

Further Reading:
Plays and Poems (Routledge, London, 1887)
The Works of George Peele (John C. Nimmo, London, 1888)
Selected Works (ed. Sally Purcell, Carcanet Press, Oxford, 1972)
David H. Home, *The Life and Minor Works of George Peele* (Yale University Press, New Haven, 1952)
A.R. Braunmuller: *George Peele* (Twayne Publ., New York, 1983)

from **The Love of King David and Fair Bathsheba,**

Prologue

Of Israel's sweetest singer now I sing,
His holy style and happy victories,
Whose muse was dipped in that inspiring dew,
Archangels stilled from the breath of Jove,
Decking, her ternples with the glorious flowers,
Heavens reigned on tops of Syon and Mount Sinai.
Upon the bosom of his ivory lute,
The cherubims and angels laid their breasts,
And when his consecrated fingers struck
The golden wires of his ravishing harp,
He gave alarum to the host of heaven,
That winged with lightning, broke the clouds and cast
Their crystal armour, at his conquering feet.
Of this sweet poet Jove's musician,
And of his beauteous son I praise to sing.
Then help divine Adonay to conduct,
Upon the wings of my well-tempered verse,
The hearers' minds above the towers of Heaven,
And guide them so in this thrice haughty flight,
Their mounting feathers scorch not with the fire,
That none can temper but thy holy hand:
To thee for succour flies my feeble muse,
And at thy feet her iron pen doth use.

He draws a curtain, and discovers Bathsheba with her maid bathing over a spring: she sings, and David sits above viewing her.

Hot sun, cool fire, tempered with sweet air,
Black shade, fair nurse, shadow my white hair.
Shine, sun; burn fire; breathe, air, and ease me;
Black shade, fair nurse, shroud me and please me;

Shadow, my sweet nurse, keep me from burning,
Make not my glad cause cause of mourning.
Let not my beauty's fire
Inflame unstaid desire,
Nor pierce any bright eye
That wand'reth lightly.

from The Arraignment of Paris

Not Iris, in her pride and bravery,
Adorns her arch with such variety;
Nor doth the milk-white way, in frosty night,
Appear so fair and beautiful in sight,
As do these fields and groves, and sweetest bowers
Bestrewed and decked with parti-coloured flowers.
Along the bubbling brooks and silver glide,
That at the bottom doth in silence slide;
The water-flowers and lilies on the banks,
Like blazing comets, burgeon all in ranks;
Under the hawthorn and the poplar tree,
Where sacred Phoebe may delight to be,
The primrose, and the purple hyacinth,
The dainty violet and the wholesome minth,
The double-daisy, and the cowslip (queen
Of summer flowers) do over-peer the green;
And round about the valley as ye pass,
Ye may not see for peeping flowers the grass.

A Song *from* The Old Wives' Tale

Whenas the rye reach to the chin,
And chop-cherry, chop-cherry ripe within,
Strawberries swimming in the cream,
And schoolboys playing in the stream;
Then, O, then, O then, O, my true love said,
Till that time come again
She could not live a maid.

Sonnet

His golden locks, time hath to silver turned,
O time too swift, O swiftness never ceasing:
His youth 'gainst time and age hath ever spurned
But spurned in vain, youth waneth by increasing.
    Beauty, strength, youth, are flowers but fading seen,
    Duty, faith, love are roots, and ever green.

His helmet, now shall make a hive for bees,
And lovers' sonnets, turned to holy psalms:
A man-at-arms must now serve on his knees,
And feed on prayers, which are age his alms:
    But though from court to cottage he depart,
    His saint is sure of his unspotted heart.

And when he saddest sits in homely cell.
He'll teach his swains this carol for a song,
"Blest be the hearts that wish my sovereign well,
Curst be the souls that think her any wrong."
    Goddess, allow this agèd man his right
    To be your beadsman now, that was your knight.

from **Polyhymnia**

Therefore, when thirty-two were come and gone,
Years of her reign, days of her country's peace,
Elizabeth great Empress of the world,
Britannia's Atlas, star of England's globe,
That sways the massy sceptre of her land,
And holds the royal reins of Albion:
Began the gladsome sunny day to shine,
That draws in length date of her golden reign:
And thirty-three she numb'reth in her throne:
That long in happiness and peace (I pray)
May number many to these thirty-three.
Wherefore it fares as whilom and of yore,
In armour bright and sheen, fair England's knights
In honour of their peerless sovereign:
High mistress of their service, thoughts and lives
Make to the tylt amain: and trumpets sound,
And princely coursers neigh, and champ the bit,
When all addressed for deeds of high devoire,
Praise to the sacred presence of their Prince.

[*tylt*: the joust; *amain*: at full speed/with haste; *devoire*: duty]

from **Polyhymnia**

The 5th couple. The Earl of Essex. M. Fulke Greville.

Then proudly shocks amid the martial throng,
Of lusty lancers, all in sable sad,
Drawn on with coal-black steeds of dusky hue,
In stately chariot full of deep device,
Where gloomy Time sat whipping on the team,
Just back to back with this great champion;
Young Essex, that thrice honourable Earl,
Yclad in mighty arms of mourner's hue,
And plume as black as is the raven's wing,
That from his armour borrowed such a light,
As bows of yew receives from shady stream,
His staves were such, or of such hue at least,
As are those banner staves that mourners bear,
And all his company in funeral black,
As if he mourned to think of him he missed,
Sweet Sidney, fairest shepherd of our green,
Well-lettered warrior, whose successor he
In love and arms had ever vowed to be.
In love and arms O may he so succeed,
As his deserts, as his desires would speed.
    With this great Lord must gallant Greville run,
Fair man at arms, the muses' favourite,
Lover of learning and of chivalry,
Sage in his saws, sound judge of poesy:
That lightly mounted, makes to him amain,
In armour gilt, and basses full of cost.
Together go these friends as enemies,
As when a lion in a thicket penned,
Spying the boar all bent to combat him,
Makes through the shrubs, and thunders as he goes.

[*yclad*: wearing]

Anne Dowriche

Anne Dowriche was born ca. 1560, the daughter of Sir Richard Edgcumbe of Mount Edgcumbe in Cornwall. At the age of 20 she married a parson, Hugh Dowriche, who was Vicar of Lapford, and later Honiton. Her only publication – and it is a rare publication by a woman in the 16th century – was *The French Historie, that is; A lamentable Discourse of three of the chiefe, and moste famous bloodie broiles that have happened in France for the Gospell of Jesus Christ. Namelie; 1. The outrage called The winning of S. James his Streete, 1557. 2. The constant Martirdome of Annas Burgeus one of the K. Councell, 1559. 3. The bloodie Marriage of Margaret Sister to Charles the 9. Anno 1572.* The events covered by the title are known today as the affair of the Rue St Jacques (1557), the Martyrdom of Annas Burgeus (1559) and the St Bartholomew's Day Massacre (1572), respectively. Her book was published in 1589, and was known to Christopher Marlowe, who seems to have used it as background material for his play *The Massacre at Paris*.

Anne Dowriche died in 1613.

Further reading:
The Early Modern Englishwoman: A Facsimile Library of Essential Works. Series 1: Printed Writings 1500-1642; Part 2, Vol. 10: The Poets I: Isabella Whitney, Anne Dowriche, Aemilia Lanyer, Rachel Speght, Diane Primrose (ed. Susanne Woods, Betty S. Travitsky and Patrick Cullen); Ashgate Publishing, Aldershot, 2001.

from The French Historie

from *The pitiful lament of a godly French exile which for persecution forsook his country: France compared with India, Egypt, and Jerusalem.*

For thou with Judah land hast done thy God great wrong,
To serve and set up other Gods to run a whoring long.
Thou hast for wooden Gods, God's lively image spilled:
And with the streams of Christian blood the streets & canals filled
Thou hast with Egypt long God's word in prison pent;
And wilfully refused the light that he to thee hath sent.
The Moses that begins this light for to unfold,
Thou seekst to lap him presently in chains and irons cold.
Thou dost with Amalek with all thy wit assay
To lie in wait that in thy land the truth may have no way.
And thou a cruel nurse to God's elect hast been,
To blemish thus the shining light that in thee hath been seen.
And with Jerusalem God's prophets thou hast slain,
That in thy popish ignorance thou mightest still remain.
If Judah shall be fed with wormwood mixed with gall;
If wilfull Egypt plagued were that kept God's church in thrall;
If God no pity showed, and mercy none would have
Upon the land of Amalek, nor man nor beast to save;
And if the blinded pride that in Jerusalem dwelt,
Could not escape God's heavy wrath, but man & child it felt.
What shall become of thee thou blind and bloody land?
How dost thou think for to escape God's just revenging hand?

The Pathetical speeches of Burgæus to the Senate of Paris at his condemnation

"Are Pluto's nymphs installed within your breast?
Doth dire Megara now possess the place where Christ should rest.
Hath Satan (which deceit and lies hath usèd long)
Enforced you against the truth and Christ to practise wrong?
And are you gone so far, that you can be content
For love ye bear to Satan's lies, to kill the innocent.
What, is there not a God that searcheth every vein?
And will he not revenge the blood of Abel spilt by Cain?
And can you now account the truth to be a lie?
And can you think within your heart that Christ can go awry?
And dare you to blaspheme that great and sacred name?
And fear you not by feignèd gloss his Gospel to defame?
And will you be so bold to say that we do stray,
Which have for us the written word, & Christ our only way?
We are the sons of God whom thus you do pursue,
If you persist, you shall too soon perceive it to be true.
We know that he doth live, his voice doth show his love:
If you refuse his proffered word, your sins shall you reprove.
By him we can do all; if he do hide his face
We may not hope without his help for mercy, love, or grace.
What boldness is it then for ashes, filth, and clay,
By fond attempt for to resist the thing that he shall say?
And can you be content that Christ for to deprave;
Whose wounds have washed our sins, whose mercy doth us save?
Shall we deny our King, our Prince, our joy, our might?
Shall we consent to do him wrong, that doth defend our right?
He is our princely Guide, our Captain, and our stay;
He wakes for us when we do sleep, & keeps us from decay.
Then hear, what shall we do? Shall fear make us to fly?
Shall any earthly force make us our Captain to deny?
Shall we unconstant be our duty to forgo?
Shall we repay such courtesy to him that loved us so?

No, no, we are but earth, to earth we must return;
O happy earth, if (earth) for Christ thou be content to burn.
Our time is here but short, our deadly foe but weak;
The Lord is able when he lift his malice for to break.
But what would Satan have? what doth this flesh require?
But only this; that from our God and truth we should retire.
If any do blaspheme, we must them not control:
If any wily wantons sin, we must their deeds extol.
If truth be trodden down: If we will live at ease,
We must be then with heavy hearts content to hold our peace.
Which sith we do refuse, you run with open cry;
Lo these are wicked rebels, which most worthy are to die.
And are we rebels then? How will your prove this thing?
Yes sir; you do refuse, with us to Baal your off'rings bring.
O mercy now good Lord! What wicked times are these?
How long shall these ungodly men keep these ungodly ways?
How long wilt thou forbear to bridle this their lust?
And when shall all their fleshly pride be rakèd in the dust?
Why dost thou wink so long? Why dost thou so delay?
Why dost thou not cut off those imps, that stir this fiery fray?
But if it be thy will that they should longer reign:
And if thou think it best for us that they should yet remain:
Restrain them yet (good Lord) least they do go too far
For they against thy godly Saints intend a cruel war.
And till thy pleasure be for to destroy them quite;
Withhold their cruel jaws (O Lord) with thy most mighty bit.
Have mercy still on us (O loving Father dear;
Maintain us in defending thee, from danger, falls and fear.
And make them Lord to know, that they those rebels are:
That from the simple (which do seek) the light & truth debar.
And while that I have breath I will declare the same;
That Satan may not with his lies thy blessèd truth defame.
Is this a rebel's part when men to Princes give
Their bodies, goods, and all things else without repine & grief?
Is this a traitor's prank unto the Lord to pray;

That he will keep both Prince & land from trouble & decay:
And that he will vouchsafe to take from them the mist
Which keeps them from the knowledge of their saviour & their
   Christ?
Or rather is not this a most rebellious part;
To seek by all rebellious means God's glory to subvert?
To give the honour due unto the Lord alone,
To saints that you have made: or else, to senseless stock & stone?
To use blasphemous oaths; to suffer common stews;
To justify your own device; and such like filthy use?
Your conscience shall be judge, to you I do appeal:
Hath God delivered you the sword against his truth to deal?
If not, beware betime, and mark what I shall say;
This malice which you bear to Christ will be your own decay.
And what, are you so blind, that you perceive not this;
How in this sentence you pronounce, that you are none of his?
Recount within your selves and call to mind at large,
Where any sin or wickedness be laid unto our charge.
If not; then judge again, and tell me if you can:
Which is the best; to serve the Lord, or follow sinful man?
Now if you love your goods, your credit, and your life;
If you prefer before your God your household, child, or wife:
Then know you are not fit with Christ to have a part;
But fear, least for your sin in hell you find a lasting smart?
But if you do not fear the judgements of the Lord:
Yet know, your deeds in foreign lands to strangers are abhorred.
How many sinful acts, and deeds devoid of wit,
That ruddy purpled Phalaris hath made you to commit?
Who for his cursèd gain hath set about the King,
Such as will Prince and Commons all to deadly ruin bring.
And when that Beast doth bid, you run at every call;
You rack & tear God's knowen truth, not caring what befall.
To please him, you do yield the godly to torment
With such outrage, as you are forced the same for to lament.
But what; me thinks I see the tears trill down your cheek?

What, have I spoken that which now your conscience doth mislike?
Well, then beware betime, for yet the time is well;
But if you shun this proffered grace, beware the pains of hell.
Your conscience must be known, your deeds must all appear.
Then call for grace, and so repent while yet you tarry here.
But if you quake in jest as Felix did before,
And if you fear without remorse your pain will be the more.
You see how they rejoice whom you condemn to die;
No terror can assail the heart on Christ that doth rely.
We weigh not all your force, your malice, and your strife;
We do account this cruel death to us a happy life.
Why should it grieve my heart for Christ to hang or burn;
For little pain, I know the Lord great pleasure will return.
But they unhappy are, and cursèd from above,
Which from themselves & others seek the truth for to remove.
But this I know from Christ nothing shall me depart,
And from assured hope in him none shall remove my heart.
For though you tear my flesh, and heart to powder grind;
Yet this shall never so prevail, as once to change my mind.
And when that you have done the worst you can devise;
We know that in the latter day with Christ we shall arise.
This death therefore to us we reckon little pain:
For we believe assuredly that we shall live again.
Now hap what may befall, to hang, to burn, to fry
I have professèd Christ: and so, a Christian I will die.
Why therefore do we stay? Come hangman do thy part;
Thy fact in this, lo here I do forgive with all my heart."
And this he did repeat, "Come hangman do the deed";
Till that the stoutest heart that heard, for grief began to bleed.
"Put out, put out" (said he) "your frantic fiery brands;
That Christ may only rule & reign, set to your helping hands.
Repent your wicked thoughts forsake your filthy ways:
And if you hope to have release, then use no more delays.
But why do I so long draw this forsaken breath?
Farewell my mates; for now behold, I go unto my death."

Joseph Hall

Joseph Hall was born in 1574 near Ashby-de-la-Zouch in Leicestershire. Hall went up to Emmanuel College, Cambridge in 1589, beginning a successful academic career and in 1595 became a fellow of his college. At Cambridge he wrote the *Virgidemiarum* (1597), one of the earliest English satires written after Latin models. The Archbishop of Canterbury ordered that Hall's satires should be burned along with the works of Marston, Marlowe and others, but they were reprieved soon after.

After taking holy orders, Hall was offered the mastership of Blundell's School in Tiverton, but declined it in favour of the living of Halsted in Essex. His devotional writings attracted the notice of Henry, Prince of Wales, who made him one of his chaplains in 1608. The King nominated him Dean of Worcester. In 1624 he declined the see of Gloucester, but in 1627 accepted the bishopric of Exeter.

He took an active part in the theological controversies of his day but fell afoul of Archbishop Laud, who sent spies to Hall's diocese. Hall, and his poetry, went on to suffer attack from John Milton.

In 1641 Hall was moved to the see of Norwich. On December 30 of that year he was, with other bishops, brought before the House of Lords to answer charges of high treason, of which the House of Commons had voted them guilty. They were convicted on a lesser charge, and forfeited their estates, receiving instead a small maintenance from Parliament. They were locked in the Tower for several months and, after being released, Hall went to his new diocese at Norwich, but his property was seized in 1643. He and his wife were ejected from the palace, and the cathedral was torn down. Hall then retired to the village of Heigham, near Norwich, where he preached until forbidden to do so. He died in 1656.

Further Reading:
The Collected Poems of Joseph Hall (ed. A Davenport; Liverpool University Press, 1949)

from **Virgidemiarum**

Satire 3

With some pot-fury ravished from their wit,
They sit and muse on some no-vulgar writ:
As frozen dunghills in a winter's morn,
That void of vapours seemed all beforn,
Soon as the sun, sends out his piercing beams,
Exhale out filthy smoke and stinking steams:
So doth the base, and the fore-barren brain,
Soon as the raging wine begins to reign.
One higher pitched doth set his soaring thought
On crownèd kings that fortune hath low brought:
Or some uprearèd, high-aspiring swain
As it might be the Turkish Tamburlaine.
Then weaneth he his base drink-drowned spright,
Rapt to the threefold loft of heaven's height,
When he conceives upon his feignèd stage
The stalking steps of his great personage,
Graced with hoof-cap terms and thund'ring threats
That his poor hearers' hair quite upright sets.
Such soon, as some brave-minded hungry youth,
Sees fitly frame to his wide-strainèd mouth,
He vaunts his voice upon an hired stage,
With high-set steps, and princely carriage:
Now sweeping in side robes of Royalty.
That erst did scrub in lousy brokery.
There if he can with terms Italianate,
Big-sounding sentences, and words of state,
Fair patch me up his pure iambic verse,
He ravishes the gazing scaffolders:
Then certes was the famous Cordoban
Never but half so high tragedian.
Now, least such frightful shows of fortune's fall,

And bloody tyrant's rage, should chance appal
The dead struck audience, 'midst the silent rout
Comes leaping in a self-misformèd lout,
And laughs, and grins, and frames his mimic face,
And hustles straight into the Prince's place.
Then doth the theatre echo all aloud,
With gladsome noise of that applauding crowd.
A goodly hotchpotch, when vile russettings,
Are matched with monarchs, & with mighty kings.
A goodly grace to sober tragic muse,
When each base clown, his clumsy fist doth bruise
And show his teeth in double rotten-row,
For laughter at his self-resembled show.
Meanwhile our poets in high Parliament,
Sit watching every word, and gesturement,
Like curious censors of some doughty gear,
Whispering their verdict in their fellow's ear.
Woe to the word whose margent in their scroll,
Is noted with a black condemning coal.
But if each period might the synod please,
Ho, bring the ivy boughs, and bands of bays.
Now when they part and leave the naked stage,
Gins the bare hearer in a guilty rage,
To curse and ban, and blame his lickerish eye,
That thus hath lavished his late half-penny.
Shame that the muses should be bought and sold,
For every peasant's brass, on each scaffold.

spright: spirit
Cordoban: Seneca
margent: margin
lickerish: (here) greedy

An Epitaph

Some leave their home for private discontent,
Some forcèd by compulsèd banishment.
Some for an itching lust of novel sight,
Someone for gain, some other for delight.
Thus whilst some force, some other hope bereaves,
Some leave their country, some their country leaves.
But thee no grief, force, lust, gain or delight,
Exilèd from thy home (thrice worthy knight)
Save that grief, force, that gain, delight alone,
Which was thy good, and true religion.

To the Praise of the Dead, and The Anatomy.
*(printed amongst the prefatory poems to
John Donne's* Anniversaries*)*

Well died the world, that we might live to see
This world of wit, in his anatomy:
No evil wants his good: so wilder heirs
Bedew their fathers' tombs with forcèd tears,
Whose state requites their loss: whilst thus we gain,
Well may we walk in blacks, but not complain.
Yet, how can I consent the world is dead
While this muse lives? which in his spirit's stead
Seems to inform a world: and bids it be,
In spite of loss, or frail mortality?
And thou the subject of this well-born thought,
Thrice noble maid; couldst not have found nor sought
A fitter time to yield to thy sad fate,
Than while this spirit lives; that can relate
Thy worth so well to our last nephew's eyne,
That they shall wonder both at his, and thine:
Admired match! where strives in mutual grace
The cunning pencil, and the comely face:
A task, which thy fair goodness made too much
For the bold pride of vulgar pens to touch;
Enough is us to praise them that praise thee,
And say that but enough those praises be,
Which had'st thou lived, had hid their fearful head
From th'angry checkings of thy modest red:
Death bars reward & shame: when envy's gone,
And gain; 'tis safe to give the dead their own.
As then the wise Egyptians wont to lay
More on their tombs, than houses: these of clay,
But those of brass, or marble were; so we
Give more unto thy ghost, than unto thee.
Yet what we give to thee, thou gav'st to us,

And may'st but thank thy self, for being thus:
Yet what thou gav'st, and wert, O happy maid,
Thy grace professed all due, where 'tis repaid.
So these high songs that to thee suited bine,
Serve but to sound thy makers praise, in thine,
Which thy dear soul as sweetly sings to him
Amid the choir of saints and seraphim,
As any angel's tongue can sing of thee;
The subjects differ, though the skill agree:
For as by infant-years men judge of age,
Thy early love, thy virtues, did presage
What an high part thou bear'st in those best songs
Whereto no burden, nor no end belongs.
Sing on, thou virgin soul, whose lossful gain
Thy love-sick parents have bewailed in vain;
Never may thy name be in our songs forgot,
Till we shall sing thy ditty, and thy note.

certes: assuredly
eyne: eyes
bine: be

John Ford

John Ford (1586-1640) was born in Ilsington, on Dartmoor, and came of a well-positioned family – his mother was the sister of Sir John Popham, Lord Chief Justice. He went up to Exeter College, Oxford, in 1601 and was admitted to the Middle Temple in 1602, although it is not clear if he ever studied Law. He was expelled from the Temple in 1606, owing to some financial problems, and from that point onwards made a living as a writer.

His first publication was an elegy, 'Fame's Memorial or the Duke of Devonshire deceased' (1606), dedicated to the Duke's widow. Although he composed poetry throughout his career, it was as a dramatist that he made his mark, working at first in collaboration with Dekker and Webster. In the 1620s and 1630s he composed all of the successful plays that we still know: *The Broken Heart, The Lover's Melancholy, Perkin Warbeck, The Witch of Edmonton*, and his masterpiece, the tragedy *'Tis Pity She's a Whore*.

Little is known of his life, other than what is in the publication record, but he is thought to have died in Devon.

Further Reading:
Fancies Chaste and Noble (1638) – replica edition, Kessinger Publishing Co., 2003.)
Tis Pity She's a Whore and Other Plays (Oxford World's Classics, Oxford University Press, 1999)

On the Best of English Poets, Ben Jonson, Deceased.

So seems a star to shoot, when from our sight
Falls the deceit, not from its loss of light;
We want use of a soul, who merely know
What to our passion or our sense we owe:
By such a hollow glass our cozened eye
Concludes alike all dead whom it sees die.
Nature is knowledge here, but unrefined,
Both differing as the body from the mind;
Laurel and cypress else had grown together,
And withered without memory to either:
Thus undistinguished might in every part
The sons of earth vie with the sons of art.
Forbid it, holy reverence, to his name,
Whose glory hath filled up the book of fame;
Where in fair capitals, free, uncontrolled,
Jonson, a work of honour, lives enrolled;
Creates that book a work; adds this far more,
'Tis finished what unperfect was before.
The Muses, first in Greece begot, in Rome
Brought forth, our best of poets have called home,
Nursed, taught, and planted here; that Thames now sings
The Delphian altars and the sacred springs.
By influence of this sovereign. Like the spheres,
Moved each by other, the most low in years
Consented in their harmony; though some,
Malignantly aspected, overcome
With popular opinion, aimed at name
More than desert: yet in despite of shame
Even they, though foiled by his contempt of wrongs,
Made music to the harshness of their songs.
      Drawn to the life of every line and limb
He – in his truth of art, and that in him –
Lives yet, and will whilst letters can be read:

The loss is ours; now hope of life is dead.
Great men and worthy of report must fall
Into their earth, and sleeping there sleep all;
Since he, whose pen in every strain did use
To drop a verse, and every verse a muse,
Is vowed to heaven; as having with fair glory
Sung thanks of honour, or some nobler story.
The court, the university, the heat
Of theatres, with what can else beget
Belief and admiration, clearly prove
Our poet first in merit as in love.
Yet if he do not as his full appear,
Survey him in his works, and know him there.

A memorial offered to that man of virtue, Sir Thomas Overbury.

Once dead and twice alive; Death could not frame
A death whose sting would kill him in his fame.
He might have lived, had not the life which gave
Life to his life betrayed him to his grave.
If greatness could consist in being good,
His goodness did add titles to his blood.
Only unhappy in his life's last fate,
In that he lived so soon, to die so late.
Alas, whereto shall men oppressèd trust,
When innocence can not protect the just?
His error was his fault, his truth his end,
No enemy his ruin but his friend:
Cold friendship, where hot vows are but a breath
To guerdon poor simplicity with death.
Was never man that felt the sense of grief
So Overbury'd in a safe belief:

Belief? O, cruel slaughter! Times unbred
Will say, who dies that is untimely dead
By treachery, of lust, or by disgrace
In friendship, 'twas but Overbury's case;
Which shall not more commend his truth than prove
Their guilt who were his opposites in love.
Rest, happy man; and in thy sphere of awe
Behold how justice sways the sword of law,
To weed out those whose hands embrewed in blood
Cropped off thy youth and flower in the bud.
Sleep in thy peace: thus happy has thou proved
Thou mightst have died more known, not more beloved.

from Epitaphs

Tomb I.

    The course of time hath finished now his breath,
Whom brunt of war could never force to death;
Whose thirst of worth the world would not suffice,
Within a breadth of earth contented lies.

Betwixt the gods and men doubly divided,
His soul with them, his fame with us abided;
In this his life and death was countervailed,
He justly lived beloved, he died bewailed.

    And so his happy memory
    Shall last to all posterity.

William Browne

William Browne – generally known as William Browne of Tavistock – was born in Tavistock around 1590. He was educated at the local grammar school and then studied at Oxford, after which he entered the Inner Temple.

The second book of his *Britannia's Pastorals* (1616) is dedicated to William Herbert, Earl of Pembroke, whose seat at Wilton was Browne's home for some time. In 1624 he returned to Oxford as tutor to Robert Dormer, later Earl of Carnarvon, matriculating at Exeter College in April and receiving his M.A. in November of the same year. Nearly all of Browne's poetic work dates from his early years, prior to his marriage in 1628 to Tymothy, the daughter of Sir Thomas Eversham. He spent the second half of his life in retirement, and appears to have died around 1643-1645, as in the latter year his wife was granted administration of his estate.

Browne was a pupil and friend of Michael Drayton, and was much influenced by Spenser's pastoral verse. His chief works were *Britannia's Pastorals* (Vol. 1., 1613; Vol. 2, 1616) and *The Shepherd's Pipe* (1614). Milton seems to have been impressed by his work, as a copy of the *Pastorals* survives, with annotations in Milton's hand. Both Herrick and Keats are thought to have been influenced by him, and in the former case, the poet's situation on the edge of Dartmoor no doubt encouraged the study of his contemporary's work, whose Arcadia is distinctly Devonian.

Further Reading:
William Browne: *The Whole Works*, Vols 1 & 2, ed. W Carew Hazlitt (1868-9)
— reprint in 1 volume: Georg Olms Verlag, Hildesheim & New York, 1970.

On a Fair Lady's Yellow Hair Powdered with White.
Written in the Dissolving of a Snow

Say, why on your hair yet stays
    That snow resembling white;
Since the sun's less powerful rays
    Thawed that which fell last night?

Sure to hinder those extremes
    Of love they might bestow;
Art hath hid your golden beams
    Within a fleece of snow.

Yet as on a cloth of gold,
    With silver flowers wrought ore,
We do now and then behold
    A radiant wire or more:

So sometimes the amorous air
    Doth with your fair locks play,
And unclouds a golden hair;
    And then breaks forth the day.

On your cheeks the rosy morn
    We plainly then descry;
And a thousand cupids born,
    And playing in each eye.

Now we all are at a stay,
    And know not where to turn us;
If we wish that snow away,
    Those glorious beams would burn us.

If it should not fall amain,
    And cloud your love-full eyes,
Each gentle heart would soon be slain,
    And made their sacrifice.

Shall I love again

Shall I love again, and try
    If I still must love to lose,
And make weak mortality
    Give new birth unto my woes?
No, let me ever live from Love's enclosing,
Rather than love to live in fear of losing.

One whom hasty Nature gives
    To the world without his sight,
Not so discontented lives,
    As a man deprived of light;
'Tis knowledge that gives vigour to our woe,
And not the want, but loss that pains us so.

With the Arabian bird then be
    Both the lover and belov'd;
Be thy lines thy progeny
    By some gracious fair approved;
So may'st thou live, and be belov'd of many,
Without the fear of loss, or want of any.

Deep are the wounds ...

Deep are the wounds which strike a virtuous name;
Sharp are the darts revenge still sets on wing:
Consuming jealousies abhorrèd flame!
Deadly the frowns of an enragèd King.
Yet all these to disdain's heart-searching string
(Deep, sharp, consuming, deadly) nothing be,
Whose darts, wounds, flames, and frowns, meet all in me.

A Rose

A rose, as fair as ever saw the north,
Grew in a little garden all alone;
A sweeter flower did nature ne'er put forth,
Nor fairer garden yet was never known:
The maidens danced about it more and more,
And learnèd bards of it their ditties made;
The nimble fairies by the pale-faced moon
Watered the root and kissed her pretty shade.
But well-a-day, the gardener careless grew;
The maids and fairies both were kept away,
And in a drought the caterpillars threw
Themselves upon the bud and every spray.
    God shield the stock! if heaven send no supplies,
    The fairest blossom of the garden dies.

from Celia: Sonnets

I.
Lo, I the man, that whilom loved & lost,
Not dreading loss, do sing again of love;
And like a man but lately tempest-tossed,
Try if my stars still inauspicious prove:
Not to make good, that poets never can
Long time without a chosen mistress be,
Do I sing thus; or my affections ran
Within the maze of mutability;
What best I loved, was beauty of the mind,
And that lodged in a temple truly fair,
Which ruined now by death, if I can find
The saint that lived therein some otherwhere,
    I may adore it there, and love the cell
    For entertaining what I loved so well.

7.
Fairest, when I am gone, as now the glass
Of time is marked how long I have to stay,
Let me entreat you, ere from hence I pass,
Perhaps from you for evermore away,
Think that no common love hath fired my breast,
No base desire, but virtue truly known,
Which I may love, & wish to have possessed,
Were you the high'st as fair'st of anyone;
'Tis not your lovely eye enforcing flames,
Nor beauteous red beneath a snowy skin,
That so much binds me yours, or makes you flames,
As the pure light & beauty shrined within:
    Yet outward parts I must affect of duty,
    As for the smell we like the rose's beauty.

A Round

Now that the Spring hath filled our veins
    With kind and active fire,
And made green liv'ries for the plains,
    And every grove a choir;

Sing we a song of merry glee,
    And Bacchus fill the bowl:
Then here's to thee; And thou to me
    And every thirsty soul.

Nor care nor sorrow ere paid debt,
    Nor never shall do mine;
I have no cradle going yet,
    Nor I, by this good wine.

No wife at home to send for me,
    No hogs are in my ground,
No suit at law to pay a fee;
    Then round, old jockey, round!

Sheer sheep that have them, cry we still,
    But see that no man 'scape
        To drink of the sherry
        That makes us so merry,
    And plump as the lusty grape

from **Britannia's Pastorals**

Gentle nymphs, be not refusing,
Love's neglect is time's abusing,
    They and beauty are but lent you,
Take the one and keep the other;
Love keeps fresh what age doth smother;
    Beauty gone, you will repent you.

'Twill be said when ye have proved,
Never swains more truly loved;
    Oh then, fly all nice behaviour.
Pity fain would, as her duty,
Be attending still on beauty,
    Let her not be out of favour.

            * * *

So shuts the marigold her leaves
    At the departure of the sun;
So from the honeysuckle sheaves
    The bee goes when the day is done;

So sits the turtle when she is but one,
And so all woe, as I since she is gone.

To some few birds kind Nature hath
    Made all the summer as one day;
Which once enjoyed, cold winter's wrath
    As night they sleeping pass away.
Those happy creatures are that know not yet
The pain to be deprived or to forget.

I oft have heard men say there be
    Some that with confidence profess
The helpful art of memory;
    But could they teach forgetfulness
I'd learn, and try what further art could do
To make me love her and forget her too.

★ ★ ★

[The Birth of the River Tavy]

As I have seen upon a bridal day
Full many maids clad in their best array,
In honour of the bride come with their flaskets
Filled full with flowers: others in wicker baskets
Bring from the marsh rushes to o'erspread
The ground whereon to church the lovers tread;
Whilst that the quaintest youth of all the plain
Ushers their way with many a piping strain:
So, as in joy at this fair river's birth,
Triton came up a channel with his mirth,
And called the neighbouring nymphs each in her turn
To pour their pretty rivulets from their urn.
To wait upon this new-delivered spring,

Some running through the meadows, with them bring
Cowslip and mint; and 'tis another's lot
To light upon some gardener's curious knot,
Whence she upon her breast, love's sweet repose,
Doth bring the queen of flowers, the English rose.
Some from the fen bring reeds, wild thyme from downs;
Some from a grove the bay that poets crowns;
Some from an agèd rock the moss hath torn,
And leaves him naked unto winter's storm;
Another from her banks, in mere goodwill,
Brings nutriment for fish, the camomile.
Thus all bring somewhat, and do overspread
The way the spring unto the sea doth tread.

Epitaph: On the Countess Dowager of Pembroke

Underneath this sable hearse
Lies the subject of all verse:
Sidney's sister, Pembroke's mother:
Death, ere thou hast slain another
Fair and learn'd and good as she,
Time shall throw a dart at thee.

Robert Herrick

Robert Herrick was born the son of a goldsmith in Cheapside, London, on 24 August, 1591. His father's early death, in 1592, led to the family's departure to the village of Hampton, Middlesex, where Herrick appears to have passed his younger years. When he turned sixteen, he was apprenticed for ten years to his uncle, Sir William Herrick, jeweller to the king, whose business was in Cheapside. He seems to have been writing at this early stage and abandoned his would-be goldsmithing career in 1613 to enter St. John's College, Cambridge, as a fellow-commoner. He was later to transfer to Trinity Hall. Some letters survive from his student days, but information about his time at Cambridge is limited. He graduated in 1617.

Herrick spent the next ten years in London, where he mixed with Ben Jonson's young poet-acolytes. A number of his lyrics date from this period. He took holy orders around 1626, and in 1627 became chaplain to the Duke of Buckingham, whom he accompanied on his unsuccessful military expedition to La Rochelle. In 1628, he was awarded the living of Dean Prior, on the edge of Dartmoor, between Exeter and Plymouth, and spent most of the rest of his life there as a parish priest, apart from an 11-year period during the Cromwellian interregnum, when he was forced out of office for political and doctrinal reasons. He is thought to have spent this period in London, surviving on the charity of friends. He died in Dean Prior in 1674.

His Collected Poems were published under the title *Hesperides* in 1648, printed in London and sold both in London and in Exeter, according to the title page. A few more poems – presumably later compositions – are extant, but his output seems to have declined after the publication, which garnered no great attention. Today he is regarded as one of the greatest lyric poets of the Caroline period.

Further Reading:
Poems of Robert Herrick (Oxford U.P., 1902; reset 1933)
Hesperides (1648) – facsimile ed, Scolar Press, Menston, 1969)
Selected Poems (ed. Tony Frazer, Shearsman Books, Exeter, 2007)
Roger B Rollin: *Robert Herrick* (Twayne Publ., New York, 1992)

The Vine

I dreamed this mortal part of mine
Was metamorphosed to a vine;
Which crawling one and every way,
Enthralled my dainty Lucia.
Me thought, her long small legs & thighs
I with my tendrils did surprise;
Her belly, buttocks, and her waist
By my soft nervelets were embraced:
About her head I writhing hung,
And with rich clusters (hid among
The leaves) her temples I behung:
So that my Lucia seemed to me
Young Bacchus ravished by his tree.
My curls about her neck did crawl,
And arms and hands they did enthrall:
So that she could not freely stir,
(All parts there made one prisoner.)
But when I crept with leaves to hide
Those parts, which maids keep unespied,
Such fleeting pleasures there I took,
That with the fancy I awoke;
And found (ah me!) this flesh of mine
More like a stock, than like a vine.

To Anthea lying in bed

So looks Anthea, when in bed she lies,
Orecome, or half betrayed by tiffanies:
Like to a twilight, or that simp'ring dawn,
That roses show, when misted o're with lawn.
Twilight is yet, till that her lawns give way;
Which done, that dawn, turns then to perfect day.

Upon Julia's Clothes

When as in silks my Julia goes,
Then, then (me thinks) how sweetly flows
That liquefaction of her clothes.

Next, when I cast mine eyes and see
That brave vibration each way free;
O how that glittering taketh me!

Delight in Disorder

A sweet disorder in the dress
Kindles in clothes a wantonness:
A lawn about the shoulders thrown
Into a fine distraction:
An erring lace, which here and there
Enthralls the crimson stomacher:
A cuff neglectful, and thereby
Ribands to flow confusedly:
A winning wave (deserving note)
In the tempestuous petticoat:
A careless shoe-string, in whose tie
I see a wild civility:
Do more bewitch me, than when art
Is too precise in every part.

Fresh Cheese and Cream

Would ye have fresh cheese and cream?
Julia's breast can give you them:
And if more; each nipple cries,
To your cream, her's strawberries.

Upon his Verses

What offspring other men have got,
The how, where, when, I question not.
These are the children I have left;
Adopted some; none got by theft.
But all are touched (like lawful plate)
And no verse illegitimate.

Kissing Usury

   Biancha, let
   Me pay the debt
I owe thee for a kiss
   Thou lend'st to me;
   And I to thee
Will render ten for this:

   If thou wilt say,
   Ten will not pay
For that so rich a one;
   I'll clear the sum,
   If it will come
Unto a million.

   By this I guess,
   Of happiness
Who has a little measure:
   He must of right,
   To th'utmost might,
Make payment for his pleasure.

No Loathsomeness in love

What I fancy, I approve,
No dislike there is in love:
Be my mistress short or tall,
And distorted therewithal:
Be she likewise one of those,
That an acre hath of nose:
Be her forehead, and her eyes
Full of incongruities:
Be her cheeks so shallow too,
As to show her tongue wag through:
Be her lips ill hung, or set,
And her grinders black as jet;
Has she thin hair, hath she none,
She's to me a paragon.

To the most virtuous Mistress Pot, who many times entertained him

When I through all my many poems look,
And see your self to beautify my book;
Me thinks that only lustre doth appear
A light fulfilling all the region here.
Gild still with flames this firmament, and be
A lamp eternal to my poetry.
Which if it now, or shall hereafter shine,
'Twas by your splendour (Lady) not by mine.
The oil was yours; and that I owe for yet:
He pays the half, who does confess the debt.

To Prince Charles upon his coming to Exeter

What fate decreed, time now has made us see
A renovation of the West by thee.
That preternatural fever, which did threat
Death to our country, now hath lost his heat:
And calms succeeding, we perceive no more
Th'unequal pulse to beat, as heretofore.
Something there yet remains for thee to do;
Then reach those ends that thou wast destined to.
Go on with Sylla's fortune; let thy fate
Make thee like him, this, that way fortunate,
Apollo's image side with thee to bless
Thy war (discreetly made) with white success.
Meantime thy prophets watch by watch shall pray;
While young Charles fights, and fighting wins the day.
That done, our smooth-paced poems all shall be
Sung in the high doxology of thee.
Then maids shall strew thee, and thy curls from them
Receive (with songs) a flow'ry diadem.

[Sylla: Lucius Cornelius Sylla, a.k.a Sulla (d. 78 BC), Consul of Rome, General and Dictator; subject of one of Plutarch's *Lives*.]

Upon a Lady fair, but fruitless

Twice has Pudica been a bride, and led
By holy Hymen to the nuptial bed.
Two youths she's known, thrice two, and twice three years;
Yet not a lily from the bed appears;
Nor will; for why, Pudica, this may know,
Trees never bear, unless they first do blow.

The Wassail

Give way, give way ye gates, and win
An easy blessing to your bin,
And basket, by our ent'ring in.

May both with manchet stand replete;
Your larders too so hung with meat,
That though a thousand, thousand eat;

Yet, ere twelve moons shall whirl about
Their silv'ry spheres, there's none may doubt,
But more's sent in, than was served out.

Next, may your dairies prosper so,
As that your pans no ebb may know;
But if they do, the more to flow.

Like to a solemn sober stream
Banked all with lilies, and the cream
Of sweetest cowslips filling them.

Then, may your plants be pressed with fruit,
Nor bee, or hive you have be mute;
But sweetly sounding like a lute.

Next may your duck and teeming hen
Both to the cocks' tread say amen;
And for their two eggs render ten.

Last, may your harrows, shares and ploughs,
Your stacks, your stocks, your sweetest mows,
All prosper by your virgin-vows.

Alas! We bless, but see none here,
That brings us either ale or beer;
In a dry-house all things are near.

Let's leave a longer time to wait,
Where rust and cobwebs bind the gate;
And all live here with needy fate.

Where chimneys do for ever weep,
For want of warmth, and stomachs keep
With noise, the servants' eyes from sleep.

It is in vain to sing, or stay
Our free-feet here; but we'll away:
Yet to the lares this we'll say,

The time will come, when you'll be sad,
And reckon this for fortune bad,
T'ave lost the good ye might have had.

[*Lares*: (Latin) the household gods]

A good Husband

A master of a house (as I have read)
Must be the first man up, and last in bed:
With the sun rising he must walk his grounds;
See this, view that, and all the other bounds:
Shut every gate; mend every hedge that's torn,
Either with old, or plant therein new thorn:
Tread o'er his glebe, but with such care, that where
He sets his foot, he leaves rich compost there.

A Nuptial Verse to Mistress Elizabeth Lee, now Lady Tracy

Spring with the lark, most comely bride, and meet
Your eager bridegroom with auspicious feet.
The morn's far spent; and the immortal sun
Corals his cheek, to see those rites not done.
Fie, lovely maid! Indeed you are too slow,
When to the temple love should run, not go.
Despatch your dressing then; and quickly wed:
Then feast, and coy't a little; then to bed.
This day is love's day; and this busy night
Is yours, in which you challenged are to fight
With such an armed, but such an easy foe,
As will if you yield, lie down conquered too.
The field is pitched; but such must be your wars,
As that your kisses must out-vie the stars.
Fall down together vanquished both, and lie
Drowned in the blood of rubies there, not die.

His Confession

Look how our foul days do exceed our fair;
And as our bad, more then our good works are:
Ev'n so those lines, penned by my wanton wit,
Treble the number of these good I've writ.
Things precious are least num'rous: men are prone
To do ten bad, for one good action.

The meadow verse or Anniversary to Mistress Bridget Lowman.

Come with the Springtime, forth fair maid, and be
This year again, the meadow's deity.
Yet ere ye enter, give us leave to set
Upon your head this flow'ry coronet:
To make this neat distinction from the rest;
You are the prime, and princess of the feast:
To which, with silver feet lead you the way,
While sweet-breath nymphs, attend on you this day.
This is your hour; and best you may command,
Since you are Lady of this fairy land.
Full mirth wait on you; and such mirth as shall
Cherish the cheek, but make none blush at all.

The parting verse, the feast there ended

Loth to depart, but yet at last, each one
Back must now go to's habitation:
Not knowing thus much, when we once do sever,
Whether or no, that we shall meet here ever.
As for myself, since time a thousand cares
And griefs hath filled upon my silver hairs;
'Tis to be doubted whether I next year,
Or no, shall give ye a re-meeting here.
If die I must, then my last vow shall be,
You'll with a tear or two, remember me,
Your sometime poet; but if fates do give
Me longer date, and more fresh springs to live:
Oft as your field, shall her old age renew,
Herrick shall make the meadow-verse for you.

His Lachrimæ or Mirth, turned to mourning

    Call me no more,
    As heretofore,
The music of a feast;
    Since now (alas)
    The mirth, that was
In me, is dead or ceased.

    Before I went
    To banishment
Into the loathèd West;
    I could rehearse
    A lyric verse,
And speak it with the best.

    But time (ay me)
    Has laid, I see
My organ fast asleep;
    And turned my voice
    Into the noise
Of those that sit and weep.

His Meditation upon Death

Be those few hours, which I have yet to spend,
Blest with the meditation of my end:
Though they be few in number, I'm content;
If otherwise, I stand indifferent:
Nor makes it matter, Nestor's years to tell,
If man lives long, and if he live not well.
A multitude of days still heapèd on,
Seldom brings order, but confusion.

Might I make choice, long life should be withstood;
Nor would I care how short it were, if good:
Which to effect, let ev'ry passing bell
Possess my thoughts, next comes my doleful knell:
And when the night persuades me to my bed,
I'll think I'm going to be buried:
So shall the blankets which come over me,
Present those turfs, which once must cover me:
And with as firm behaviour I will meet
The sheet I sleep in, as my winding-sheet.
When sleep shall bathe his body in mine eyes,
I will believe, that then my body dies:
And if I chance to wake, and rise thereon,
I'll have in mind my resurrection,
Which must produce me to that gen'ral doom,
To which the peasant, so the prince must come,
To hear the judge give sentence on the throne,
Without the least hope of affection.
Tears, at that day, shall make but weak defence;
When hell and horror fright the conscience.
Let me, though late, yet at the last, begin
To shun the least temptation to a sin;
Though to be tempted be no sin, until
Man to th'alluring object gives his will.
Such let my life assure me, when my breath
Goes thieving from me, I am safe in death;
Which is the height of comfort, when I fall,
I rise triumphant in my funeral.

William Strode

William Strode was born in Plympton, Devon, in 1602, the only son of Philip Strode, who came of a Devon family of long standing. From an early age he showed an aptitude for his studies and was sent to Westminster School and then Oxford. While at the University he began to write poetry, and generally distinguished himself, being elected Public Orator in 1629. He took orders and became chaplain to Richard Corbet when the latter became Bishop of Oxford. Later he was Rector of E. Bredenham, Norfolk, and of Badley, Northants, and Canon of Christ Church.

On the outbreak of the Civil War he supported the King. He was a High Churchman, and had a reputation as "a witty and sententious preacher, an exquisite orator, and an eminent poet." His play, *The Floating Island*, a political allegory, was produced in 1633 and played before the Court – then on a visit to Oxford – where it was a subject of complaint that it "had more moralising than amusement". He died in 1645. His work was not collected in book form until 1907 (see below).

Further Reading:
The Poetical Works of William Strode (Bertram Dobell, London, 1907)
Selected Poems (Shearsman Books, Exeter, 2008)

In Commendation of Music

When whispering strains do softly steal
With creeping passion through the heart,
And when at every touch we feel
Our pulses beat and bear a part;
    When threads can make
    A heartstring shake
    Philosophy
    Can scarce deny
The soul consists of harmony.

When unto heavenly joy we feign
Whatere the soul affecteth most,
Which only thus we can explain
By music of the wingèd host,
    Whose lays we think
    Make stars to wink,
    Philosophy
    Can scarce deny
Our souls consist of harmony.

O lull me, lull me, charming air,
My senses rock with wonder sweet;
Like snow on wool thy fallings are,
Soft, like a spirit's, are thy feet:
    Grief who need fear
    That hath an ear?
    Down let him lie
    And slumb'ring die,
And change his soul for harmony.

Song

Keep on your mask, and hide your eye,
For with beholding you I die:
Your fatal beauty, Gorgon-like,
Dead with astonishment will strike;
Your piercing eyes if them I see
Are worse than basilisks to me.

Shut from mine eyes those hills of snow,
Their melting valleys do not show;
Their azure paths lead to despair,
O vex me not, forbear, forbear;
For while I thus in torments dwell
The sight of heaven is worse than hell.

Your dainty voice and warbling breath
Sound like a sentence passed for death;
Your dangling tresses are become
Like instruments of final doom.
O if an angel torture so,
When life is done where shall I go?

Upon the Blush of a Fair Lady

Stay lusty blood! Where canst thou seek
So blest a seat as in her cheek?
How dar'st thou from her face retire
Whose beauty doth command desire?
But if thou wilt not stay, then flow
Down to her panting paps below:
There take thou glory to distain
With azure blue each swelling vein,

From thence run boiling through each part
Till thou hast warmed her frozen heart,
Which, if from love thou find'st entire,
O martyr it with gentle fire.

    [*distain*: stain, discolour]

To a Gentlewoman for a Friend

No marvel if the sun's bright eye
Shower down hot flames; that quality
Still waits on light; but when we see
Those sparkling balls of ebony
Distill such heat, the gazer straight
Stands so amazed at the sight
As when the lightning makes a breach
Through pitchy clouds: can lightning reach
The marrow hurting not the skin?
Your eyes to me the same have been;
Can jet invite the loving straw
With secret fire? So those can draw,
And can, where ere they glance a dart,
Make stubble of the strongest heart.
Oft when I look I may descry
A little face peep through your eye;
Sure 'tis the boy, who wisely chose
His throne among such rays as those,
Which, if his quiver chance to fail,
May serve for darts to kill withal:
If to such powerful shafts I yield,
If with so many wounds I bleed,
Think me no coward, though I lie
Thus prostrate with your charming eye:
Did I say but your eye? I swear
Death's in your beauty everywhere.

Your waxen hands when I recall,
Your lily breasts, their melting vale,
Your damask cheeks, your lily skin,
Your coral lip and dainty chin,
Your shining locks and amber breath,
All pleasing instruments of death,
Your eye may spare itself: mine own
When all your parts are duly known
From any part may fetch a dart
To wound itself. Kill not my heart,
By saying that I will despise
The parentage from which you rise:
I know it well, and likewise know
That I myself my breath do owe
To Wolsey's roof, and can it be
I should disdain your pedigree?
Or is your sire a butcher found?
The fitter you to make a wound;
Wound me again and more and more,
So you again will me restore,
But if resemblance tell the father
I think he was an angel rather.

Song: *A Strange Gentlewoman*
         Passing By His Window

As I out of a casement sent
Mine eyes as wand'ring as my thought,
Upon no certain object bent,
But only what occasion brought,
A sight surprised my heart at last,
Nor knew I well what made it burn;
Amazement held me then so fast
I had no leisure to discern.

Sure 'twas a mortal, but her name,
Or happy parentage or place,
Or (that which did me most inflame)
I cannot tell her very face:
No; 'twere profane to think I could,
And I should pitch my thoughts too low
If ever set my love I should
On that which art or words can show.

Was ever man so vexed before,
Or ever love so blind as this,
Which vows and wishes to implore,
And yet not knows for what to wish?
Thus children spend their wayward cries,
Not knowing why they do complain;
Thus sick men long for remedies,
Not knowing what would ease their pain.

Some god call back again that sight;
I'll suffer double pain to boot,
For grief and anger in me fight
So strongly at no mark to shoot!
Not only means to win her grace,
But means to seek are barred from me;
Despair enforced by such a case
Is not a sin but misery.

Pygmalion hold thine image fast,
'Tis something to enjoy love so:
Narcissus thou a shadow hast,
At least thereby to cheat thy woe;
But I no likeness can infer
My pining fancy to supply;
Nothing to love instead of her
For fear of some idolatry.

On a Gentlewoman's Blistered Lip

Hide not that sprouting lip, nor kill
The juicy bloom with bashful skill:
Know it is an amorous dew
That swells to court thy coral hue,
And what a blemish you esteem
To other eyes a pearl may seem
Whose watery growth is not above
The thrifty size that pearls do love,
And doth so well become that part
That chance may seem a secret art.
Doth any judge that face less fair
Whose tender silk a mole doth bear?
Or will a diamond shine less clear
If in the midst a soil appear?
Or else that eye a finer net
Whose glass is ringed about with jet?
Or is an apple thought more sweet
When honey specks and red do meet?
    Then is the lip made fairer by
    Such sweetness of deformity.
The nectar which men strive to sip
Springs like a well upon your lip,
Nor doth it show immodesty,
But overflowing chastity.
O who will blame the fruitful trees
When too much sap and gum he sees?
Here nature from her store doth send
Only what other parts can lend;
The bud of love which here doth grow
Were too too sweet if plucked below;
When lovely buds ascend so high
The root below cannot be dry.

For a Gentleman, Who, Kissing His Friend at His Departure Left a Sign of Blood on Her

What mystery was this; that I should find
My blood in kissing you to stay behind?
'Twas not for want of colour that required
My blood for paint: no die could be desired
On that fair silk, where scarlet were a spot
And where the juice of lilies but a blot.
'Twas not the sign of murder that did taint
The harmless beauty of so pure a saint:
Yes, of a loving murder, which rough steel
Could never work; such as we joy to feel:
Whereby the ravished soul though dying lives,
Since life and death the selfsame object gives.
If at the presence of a murderer
The wound will bleed and tell the cause is there,
A touch will do much more, and thus my heart,
When secretly it felt the killing dart,
Showed it in blood: which yet doth more complain
Because it cannot be so touched again.
This wounded heart, to show its love most true,
Sent forth a drop and writ its mind on you.
Never was paper half so white as this,
Nor wax so yielding to the printed kiss,
Nor sealed so strong. No letter ere was writ
That could the author's mind so truly hit.
For though myself to foreign countries fly,
My blood desires to keep you company.
Here could I spill it all: thus I can free
Mine enemy from blood, though slain I be:
But slain I cannot be, nor meet with ill,
Since but by you I have no blood to spill.

A Parallel Between Bowling and Preferment

Preferment, like a game at bowls,
To feed our hope with diverse play
Here quick it runs, there soft it rolls:
The betters make and show the way.

As upper ground, so great allies
Do many cast on their desire:
Some up are thrust, and forced to rise,
When those are stopped that would aspire.

Some whose heat and zeal exceed
Thrive well by rubs that curb their hast
Some that languish in their speed
Are cherished by a gentle blast.

Some rest: and others cutting out
The same by whom themselves were made:
Some fetch a compass far about
And secretly the mark invade.

Some get by knock, and so advance
Their fortune by a boist'rous aim:
And some who have the sweetest chance
Their mistress hit, and win the game.

The fairest casts are those that owe
No thanks to fortune's giddy sway:
Such honest men good bowls do throw,
Whose own true bias cuts the way.

To His Mistress

In your stern beauty I can see
Whatere in Etna wonders be;
If coals out of the top do fly
Hot flames do gush out of your eye;
If frost lie on the ground below
Your breast is white and cold as snow:
The sparks that set my heart on fire
Refuse to melt your own desire:
The frost that binds your chilly breast
With double fire hath me oppressed:
Both heat and cold a league have made,
And leaving you they me invade:
The hearth its proper flame withstands
When ice itself heats others' hands.

A Lover to His Mistress

I'll tell you how the rose did first grow red,
And whence the lily whiteness borrowèd:
You blushed, and then the rose with red was dight:
The lilies kissed your hands, and so came white:
Before that time each rose had but a stain,
The lily nought but paleness did contain:
You have the native colour, these the dye;
They flourish only in your livery.

Love Compared to a Game of Tables

Love is a game at tables where the die
Of maids' affections doth by fancy fly:
If once you catch their fancy in a blot
It's ten to one if then you enter not:
You being a gamester then may boldly venter,
And if you find the point lie open enter:
But mark them well, for by false playing then,
Do what you can they will be bearing men.

[*venter*: venture]

A Devonshire Song

Thou ne're wutt riddle, neighbour Jan
    Where Ich a late ha been-a?
Why ich ha been at Plymouth, man,
    The leek was yet ne're zeen-a.
Zutch streetes, zutch men, zutch hugeous zeas,
    Zutch things with guns there rumbling.
Thy zelfe leek me thoudst bless to see,
    Zutch overmonstrous grumbling.

The town orelaid with shindle stone
    Doth glisten like the skee-a:
Brave shops stand ope, and all year long
    I think a fair there bee-a:
A many gallant man there goth
    In gold that zaw the King-a;
The King zome zwear himzelf was there,
    A man or zome zutch thing-a.

Voole thou that hast no water past,
    But thicka in the moore-a,
To zee the zea would be aghast,
    It doth zo rage and roar-a:
Zo zalt it tastes thy tongue will think
    The vier is in the water;
It is zo wide no land is spied,
    Look ne're zo long thereafter.

The water vrom the element
    None can dezeive cha vore-a,
It semmeth low, yet all consent
    'Tis higher than the moore-a.
'Tis strange how looking down the cliff
    Men look mere upward rather;
If these same een had it not zeen
    Chud scarce believe my vather.

Amid the water wooden birds,
    And vlying houses zwimm-a,
All vull of goods as ich have heard
    And men up to the brimm-a:
They venter to another world
    Desiring to conquier-a,
Vor which their guns, voul devilish ons,
    Do dunder and spit vier-a.

Good neighbour Tom, how far is that?
    This meazell town chill leave-a;
Chill mope no longer here, that's vlat
    To watch a sheep or shear-a:
Though it as var as London be,
    Which ten mile ich imagin,
Chill thither hie for this place I
    Do take in great indulgin.

Sidney Godolphin

Sidney Godolphin was the son of Sir William Godolphin of Godolphin in Cornwall, and of Thomasine Sidney. He was born in January 1610, and studied at Exeter College, Oxford University, from 1624. He became MP for Helston at the age of eighteen, and fought under Hopton in the Civil War, on the Royalist side. He was killed in a skirmish at Chagford on 10 February, 1643, and was buried in Okehampton.

He had a minor reputation as a poet in his own day, but his work was only collected in 1931, when Oxford University Press issued the *Poems* in an edition by William Dighton. The main sources for this edition were two manuscripts, Malone 39 at the Bodleian Library and Harleian 1917 in the British Library. Godolphin had not achieved a great deal in poetry at the time of his death, but his lyric poems stand up well by comparison with his contemporaries and one can only regret his loss at an early age.

Further Reading:
Poems (ed. W. Dighton, Oxford U.P., 1931).

Chorus

Vain man, born to no happiness,
but by the title of distress,
Allied to a capacity
of joy, only by misery;
whose pleasures are but remedies,
and best delights but the supplies
of what he wants, who hath no sense
but poverty and indigence:
Is it not pain still to desire
and carry in our breast this fire?
Is it not deadness to have none,
and satisfied, are we not stone?
Doth not our chiefest bliss then lie
Betwixt thirst and satiety,
in the mid way? which is alone
in an half satisfaction:
and is not love the middle way,
at which, with most delight we stay?
Desire is total indigence,
But love is ever a mixed sense
of what we have, and what we want,
and though it be a little scant
of satisfaction, yet we rest
in such an half possession best.
A half possession doth supply
the pleasure of variety,
and frees us from inconstancy
by want caused, or satiety;
He never loved, who doth confess
he wanted all he doth possess,
(Love to itself is recompense
besides the pleasure of the sense)·
And he again, who doth pretend

that surfeited his love took end,
Confesses in his love's decay
his soul more mortal, than that clay
which carries it, for if his mind
be in its purest part confined,
(for such love is) and limited,
'tis in the rest, dying, or dead:
they pass their times in dreams of love
whom wavering passions gently move,
through a calm smooth-faced sea they pass,
but in the haven traffic glass:
they who love truly through the clime
of freezing North and scalding line,
Sail to their joys, and have deep sense
both of the loss, and recompense:
yet strength of passion doth not prove
Infallibly, the truth of love,
Ships, which today a storm did find,
are since becalmed, and feel no wind.

Song

Or love me less, or love me more
    and play not with my liberty,
Either take all, or all restore,
    bind me at least, or set me free,
Let me some nobler torture find
    than of a doubtful wavering mind,
take all my peace, but you betray
    mine honour too this cruel way.

'Tis true that I have nursed before
    that hope of which I now complain
and having little sought no more,

      fearing to meet with your disdain:
the sparks of favour you did give,
      I gently blew to make them live:
and yet have gained by all this care
      no rest in hope, nor in despair.

I see you wear that pitying smile
      which you have still vouchsafed my smart,
Content thus cheaply to beguile
      and entertain an harmless heart:
But I no longer can give way
      to hope, which doth so little pay,
And yet I dare no freedom owe
      whilst you are kind, though but in show.

Then give me more, or give me less,
      do not disdain a mutual sense
or your unpitying beauties dress
      in their own free indifference
But show not a severer eye
      sooner to give me liberty,
for I shall love the very scorn
      which for my sake you do put on.

No more unto my thoughts appear

No more unto my thoughts appear
      at least appear less fair
For crazy tempers justly fear
      the goodness of the air;

Whilst your pure image hath a place
      in my impurer mind

your very shadow is the glass
    Where my defects I find.

Shall I not fly that brighter light
    which makes my fires look pale
and put that virtue out of sight
    which makes mine none at all.

No, no, your picture doth impart
    Such value I not wish
the native worth to any heart
    that's unadorned with this.

Though poorer in desert I make
    myself whilst I admire
the fuel which from hope I take
    I give to my desire.

If this flame lighted from your eyes
    the subject do calcine
A heart may be your sacrifice
    too weak to be your shrine.

That you may see your letters use

Sir
That you may see your letters use
both to transfer your verse, and muse,
and bring with them so fresh a heat
able new poems to beget,
(Yet such as may no more compare
with yours, than echoing voices dare)
I from my prose and Friday time

cannot but send thus much in rhyme;
Sir your grave author had no cause
to give our sense of seeing, laws,
for sure ill eyes will sooner need
Medicines, to judge of greyhounds' speed,
than other rules, since who is he
so inward blind as not to see
that overtaking going by,
Doth clearly show where odds doth lie,
Nor hath the eye an object more
distinct than this, in all its power,
All judgment else (I think) but this
A little too uncertain is,
To overrule a favouring eye
and partial minds to satisfy,
And I count nothing victory,
But when all clamour too doth die;
In all romances, the good knight
with monsters (after men) doth fight
Then you have fully got the field
When Philip and James white do yield,
So likewise nothing can adorn
our triumph, but your captive horn,
You have no cause to fear that we
Will still appeal to Salisbury,
the paddock course, and dieting,
shall we for wanton say a thing
which for the worst cur might be said
which ever yet in slip was lead,
No, from a straight course at the hare
Lies no appeal at any bar;
In one thing only I foresee
Wanton will still unhappy be,
Snap will live in your poetry
When wanton and my verses die.

Elegy on D.D. [Dr. Donne]

Now, by one year, time and our frailty have
Lessened our first confusion, since the grave
Closed thy dear ashes, and the tears which flow
In these, have no springs, but of solid woe:
Or they are drops, which cold amazement froze
At thy decease, and will not thaw in prose:
All streams of verse which shall lament that day,
Do truly to the Ocean tribute pay;
But they have lost their saltness, which the eye
In recompense of wit, strives to supply:
Passion's excess for thee we need not fear,
Since first by thee our passions hallowed were;
Thou mad'st our sorrows, which before had been
Only for the success, sorrows for sin,
We owe thee all those tears, now thou art dead,
Which we shed not, which for ourselves we shed.
Nor didst thou only consecrate our tears,
Give a religious tincture to our fears;
But even our joys had learned an innocence,
Thou didst from gladness separate offence:
All minds at once sucked grace from thee, as where
(The curse revoked) the nations had one ear.
Pious dissector: thy one hour did treat
The thousand mazes of the heart's deceit;
Thou didst pursue our loved and subtle sin,
Through all the foldings we had wrapped it in,
And in thine own large mind finding the way
By which ourselves we from ourselves convey,
Didst in us, narrow models, know the same
Angles, though darker, in our meaner frame.
How short of praise is this? My muse, alas,
Climbs weakly to that truth which none can pass,
He that writes best, may only hope to leave

A character of all he could conceive
But none of thee, and with me must confess,
That fancy finds some check, from an excess
Of merit most, of nothing, it hath spun,
And truth, as reason's task and theme, doth shun.
She makes a fairer flight in emptiness,
Than when a bodied truth doth her oppress.
Reason again denies her scales, because
Hers are but scales, she judges by the laws
Of weak comparison, thy virtue sleights
Her feeble beam, and her unequal weights.
What prodigy of wit and piety
Hath she else known, by which to measure thee?
Great soul: we can no more the worthiness
Of what you were, than what you are, express.

On Ben Jonson

The muses' fairest light in no dark time,
The wonder of a learnèd age; the line
Which none can pass; the most proportioned wit,
To nature, the best judge of what was fit;
The deepest, plainest, highest, clearest pen;
The voice most echoed by consenting men,
The soul which answered best to all well said
By others, and which most requital made,
Tuned to the highest key of ancient Rome,
Returning all her music with his own,
In whom with nature, study claimed a part,
And yet who to himself owed all his art:
    Here lies Ben Jonson, every Age will look
    With sorrow here, with wonder on his book.

Mary, Lady Chudleigh

Born Mary Lee in 1656 at Winslade, near Clyst St Mary, four miles from Exeter, she married Sir George Chudleigh, whose family seat was at Ashton, some ten miles west of Exeter.

A woman of staunch Protestant views, Mary was self-educated in religious, scientific, and philosophical works. She was close friends with John Dryden, the leading poet of the age, and was part of an intellectual circle that included Mary Astell, Elizabeth Thomas and Lady Mary Wortley Montagu. Dryden was a frequent visitor to the area and stayed with the Chudleighs.

Regarded today, with some justification, as a proto-feminist, Lady Chudleigh was the author of three works published in her own lifetime: *The Ladies' Defence, Or, a Dialogue Between Sir John Brute, Sir William Loveall, Melissa, and a Parson* (1701), *Poems on Several Occasions* (1703), and *Essays Upon Several Subjects* (1710). It has been suggested that her husband may have been the role model for the boorish Sir John Brute in *The Ladies' Defence*, but this is cast into doubt by the fact that he permitted her to publish these works during his lifetime and further permitted them to be reprinted after his wife's death in 1710.

Lady Chudleigh only began to publish ten years before her death, but her works were reprinted several times and continued to find favour throughout the subsequent centuries. Today she is recognised as a significant figure of the period.

Further Reading:
The Poems and Prose of Mary, Lady Chudleigh (ed. Margaret J.M. Ezell, Oxford University Press, New York, 1993).
Selected Poems (Shearsman Books, Exeter, 2008)
George Ballard: *Memoirs of Several Ladies of Great Britain who have been Celebrated for their Writings or Skill in the Learned Languages, Arts and Sciences* (ed. Ruth Perry, Wayne State University Press, Detroit, 1985).
Eighteenth-Century Women Poets: An Oxford Anthology (ed. Roger Lonsdale, Oxford University Press, New York, 1989).

To the Ladies

Wife and servant are the same,
But only differ in the name:
For when that fatal knot is tied,
Which nothing, nothing can divide:
When she the word *obey* has said,
And man by law supreme has made,
Then all that's kind is laid aside,
And nothing left but state and pride:
Fierce as an eastern prince he grows,
And all his innate rigour shows:
Then but to look, to laugh, or speak,
Will the nuptial contract break.
Like mutes she signs alone must make,
And never any freedom take:
But still be governed by a nod,
And fear her husband as her God:
Him still must serve, him still obey,
And nothing act, and nothing say,
But what her haughty Lord thinks fit,
Who with the pow'r, has all the wit.
Then shun, oh! shun that wretched state,
And all the fawning flatt'rers hate:
Value yourselves, and men despise,
You must be proud, if you'll be wise.

On the Death of his Highness the Duke of Gloucester
(excerpts)
1.
I'll take my leave of business, noise and care,
    And trust this stormy sea no more:
    Condemned to toil, and fed with air,

    I've often sighing looked towards the shore:
        And when the boist'rous winds did cease,
        And all was still, and all was peace,
        Afraid of calms, and flatt'ring skies,
On the deceitful waves I fixed my eyes,
And on a sudden saw the threat'ning billows rise:
        Then trembling begged the Pow'rs Divine,
Some little safe retreat might be for ever mine:
        O give, I cried, where e'er you please,
        Those gifts which mortals prize,
        Grown fond of privacy and ease,
I now the gaudy pomps of life despise.
        Still let the greedy strive with pain,
        T'augment their shining heaps of clay;
        And punished with the thirst of gain,
        Their honour lose, their conscience stain:
        Let th'ambitious thrones desire
        And still with guilty haste aspire;
        Through blood and dangers force their way,
        And o'er the world extend their sway,
While I my time to nobler uses give,
And to my books, and thoughts entirely live;
Those dear delights, in which I still shall find
        Ten thousand joys to feast my mind,
Joys, great as sense can bear, from all its dross refined.

2.
    The muse well pleased, my choice approved,
    And led me to the shades she loved:
    To shades, like those first famed abodes
    Of happy men, and rural gods;
    Where, in the world's blest infant state,
    When all in friendship were combined
    And all were just, and all were kind;
    E're glitt'ring show'rs, dispersed by Jove,

And gold were made the price of love,
The nymphs and swains did bless their fate,
And all their mutual joys relate,
Danced and sung, and void of strife.
Enjoyed all harmless sweets of life;
While on their tuneful reeds their poets played,
And their chaste loves to future times conveyed.

3.
Cool was the place, and quiet as my mind,
　The sun could there no entrance find:
　No ruffling winds the boughs did move:
　The waters gently crept along,
　As with their flow'ry banks in love:
　The birds with soft harmonious strains,
　　　Did entertain my ear;
　Sad Philomela sung her pains,
　　　Expressed her wrongs, and her despair;
　I listened to her mournful song,
　　　　　The charming warbler pleased,
And I, me thought, with new delight was seized:
Her voice with tender'st passions filled my breast,
And I felt raptures not to be expressed;
　Raptures, till that soft hour unknown,
　My soul seemed from my body flown:
Vain world, said I, take, take my last adieu,
I'll to my self, and to my muse be true,
And never more fantastic forms pursue:
Such glorious nothings let the great adore,
　Let them their airy Juno's court,
　　　I'll be deceived no more,
　Nor to the marts of fame resort:
From this dear solitude no more remove,
But here confine my joy, my hope, my love.

The Happy Man

He is the happy man whose constant mind
Is to th' enjoyment of himself confined:
Who has within laid up a plenteous store,
And is so rich that he desires no more:
Whose soul is always easy, firm, and brave,
And much too great to be ambition's slave:
Who fortune's frowns without concern can bear,
And thinks it less to suffer, than to fear:
Who, still the same, keeps up his native state,
Unmoved at all the menaces of fate:
Who all his passions absolutely sways,
And to his reason cheerful homage pays,
Who's with a halcyon calmness ever blest,
With inward joy, untroubled peace, and rest:
Who while the most with toil, with guilt, and heat,
Lose their dear quiet to be rich and great,
Both business, and disturbing crowds does shun,
Pleased that his work is with less trouble done:
To whom a grove, a garden, or a field,
Much greater, much sublimer pleasures yield,
Than they can find in all the charms of pow'r,
Those splendid ills which so much time devour:
Who more than life, his friends and books can prize,
And for those joys the noisy world despise:
Who when death calls, no weakness does betray,
Nor to an unbecoming fear give way;
But to himself, and to his maxims true,
Lies smiling down, and bids mankind adieu.

from **To the Learned and Ingenious
  Dr. Musgrave of Exeter**

1.
Those who like me their gratitude would show,
    Are grieved to think they still must owe:
Be still obliged, and never know the way
The smallest part of the vast sum to pay:
A sum beyond th' arithmetic of thought,
    And which does daily higher rise:
To be your debtor is no more my fault,
The whole that I can give, will not suffice:
    I am too poor returns to make,
Unless you'll thanks as a requital take:
    Thanks are the whole that I can bring:
My muse shall of your wondrous bounty sing;
Your gen'rous temper to the world make known,
That gen'rous temper you've so often shown,
And which I still must with the highest praises own.

2.
    But what, alas, is it I say!
Can I with thanks for a loved daughter pay?
Can her dear life that's owing to your care,
Any proportion to such trifles bear?
With weeping eyes I saw her fainting lie,
      Gasping for breath,
    But saw no safety nigh.
As some poor wretch who from the distant shore,
And with insulting waves quite covered o'er,
With piteous cries does for assistance pray,
    And strives t' escape the liquid death;
Thus almost lost your helpless patient lay,
To the devouring waters left a prey,
    Till she was rescued by your hand:

By such amazing skill, and depth of thought,
Once more into the number of the living brought:
Where she the trophy of your art does stand,
That pow'rful art, which hitherto does save
A life, which long since seemed determined to the grave.

3.
    Under your care while she remained,
    Each day she strength and spirits gained:
    Her health such quick advances made,
That all with wonder did its progress view,
And when they looked on her, applauded you:
But since she from your care was snatched away
    Like plants which want reviving rays,
        She withers in the shade,
        And hourly does decay:
    Had Heav'n designed her length of days,
    She ne'er had been from you removed,
But fate to her has inauspicious proved:
Weak as she is, she still does thanks repay,
    Does still your former favours own,
Those kindnesses you've in her sickness shown;
And in the fittest words that she can frame,
She strives to pay her homage to your fame,
And add a worthless mite to th'glory of your name.

The Fifteenth Psalm Paraphrased

Who on Thy holy hill, my God, shall rest,
And be with everlasting pleasures blessed?
The man who blameless is, and still sincere,
And who no judge does but his conscience fear:
Whose practice is a transcript of Thy law,
And whom Thy omnipresence keeps in awe:
Who speaks the truth, and would much sooner die,
Than owe his life to the loathed refuge of a lie.
Whose soul is free from falsehood and design,
And in whose words integrity does shine:
Who scorns to flatter, and by little arts
To purchase treasures, or inveigle hearts:
Who to his neighbour has no mischief done,
Does spiteful actions with abhorrence shun,
And cannot be to what's inhuman won:
Who thinks the best, and none will e'er defame,
But as his own, preserves another's name:
Who's ever humble, and is still inclined
T'inspect himself, and his own failings find:
Who loves reproofs, and a respect does pay
To those who kindly guide him in his way,
Who loves the good, those who to virtue true,
Its dictates always cheerfully pursue;
And a regard for honour in their actions shew:
Who when he swears, true to his oath will prove,
And whom nor fear, nor int'rest e'er can move,
(No, not though it to's prejudice should be,)
To disappoint his greatest enemy:
Much less, though to his ruin it should tend,
Once to deceive a kind confiding friend:
Who bravely avaricious thoughts disdains,
And is a stranger to base sordid gains:
Who'd rather starve, than th'innocent betray,

Or to base undermining thoughts give way:
He who lives thus, who this his business makes,
And never once the paths of life forsakes,
Like some strong tow'r unshaken shall remain,
And all the batteries of fate sustain.

Friendship

Friendship is a bliss divine,
And does with radiant lustre shine:
But where can that blest pair be found
That are with equal fetters bound?
Whose hearts are one, whose souls combine,
And neither know or mine, or thine;
Who've but one joy, one grief, one love,
And by the selfsame dictates move;
Who've not a frailty unrevealed,
Nor yet a thought that is concealed;
Who freely one another blame,
And strive to raise each other's fame;
Who're always just, sincere, and kind,
By virtue, not by wealth, combined;
Whose friendship nothing can abate,
Nor poverty, nor adverse fate,
Nor death itself: for when above,
They'll never, never, cease to love,
But with a passion more refined,
Become one pure celestial mind.

The Wish

Would but indulgent fortune send
To me a kind, and faithful friend,
One who to virtue's laws is true,
And does her nicest rules pursue;
One pious, lib'ral, just and brave,
And to his passions not a slave;
Who full of honour, void of pride,
Will freely praise, and freely chide;
But not indulge the smallest fault,
Nor entertain one slighting thought:
Who still the same will ever prove,
Will still instruct, and still will love:
In whom I safely may confide,
And with him all my cares divide:
Who has a large capacious mind,
Joined with a knowledge unconfined;
A reason bright, a judgment true,
A wit both quick, and solid too:
Who can of all things talk with ease,
And whose converse will ever please:
Who charmed with wit, and inward graces,
Despises fools with tempting faces;
And still a beauteous mind does prize
Above the most enchanting eyes:
I would not envy queens their state,
Nor once desire a happier fate.

John Gay

John Gay (1685-1732) was born in Barnstaple, and was orphaned at the age of ten. Thanks to his uncle, Rev. John Hanmer, he was educated at the town grammar school, and was then apprenticed to a silk merchant in London. He seems not to have liked his new trade, and left to work first for a theatre manager, and later for the Duchess of Monmouth, Lord Clarendon, and then the Ambassador to Hanover, as secretary.

In 1713, he published the comic poem 'Rural Sports' and dedicated it to Alexander Pope, who seems to have taken to both the poem and its author. Gay also developed a good relationship with Jonathan Swift, and it was at the urging of both Pope and Swift that he was to write his most successful stage work, *The Beggar's Opera* (1728). This work was an innovative 'ballad-opera', the success of which drove Italian opera from the English stage. It ran for sixty-two nights, an astonishing success for the time, and has been revived in many guises ever since. In 1716 he published *Trivia, or the Art of Walking the Streets of London*, a poem in three books, for which he acknowledged having received several tips from Swift. He also composed verse fables and — with Alexander Pope and John Hughes — co-wrote the libretto for Handel's *Acis and Galatea*.

Gay invested all his assets in South Sea Company stock, after being given some shares by a well-meaning patron, and lost everything in the ensuing Bubble. In 1722, he was given the sinecure as Lottery Commissioner at a salary of £150 a year, and from 1722 to 1729 had lodgings in the Palace at Whitehall. He continued to be lucky in his patrons: the Duke of Queensberry gave him a home, and his widow, the Duchess, continued this patronage until the author's death in 1732. He was buried in Westminster Abbey. The epitaph on his tomb is by Pope, and is followed by Gay's own lines: "Life is a jest, and all things show it, I thought so once, and now I know it."

Further Reading:
Selected Poems (ed. Marcus Walsh, Carcanet Press, Manchester, 1997)
The Beggar's Opera (ed. Loughrey & Treadwell, Penguin Classics,
    London, 1986).

An Elegy on a Lap-dog

Shock's fate I mourn; poor Shock is now no more,
Ye muses mourn, ye chamber-maids deplore.
Unhappy Shock! Yet more unhappy fair,
Doomed to survive thy joy and only care!
Thy wretched fingers now no more shall deck,
And tie the fav'rite ribbon round his neck;
No more thy hand shall smooth his glossy hair,
And comb the wavings of his pendant ear.
Yet cease thy flowing grief, forsaken maid;
All mortal pleasures in a moment fade:
Our surest hope is in an hour destroyed,
And love, best gift of heav'n, not long enjoyed.
    Me thinks I see her frantic with despair,
Her streaming eyes, wrung hands, and flowing hair
Her Mechlen pinners rent the floor bestrow,
And her torn fan gives real signs of woe.
Hence superstition, that tormenting guest,
That haunts with fancied fears the coward breast;
No dread events upon this fate attend,
Stream eyes no more, no more thy tresses rend.
Though certain omens oft forewarn a state,
And dying lions show the monarch's fate;
Why should such fears bid Celia's sorrow rise?
For when a lap-dog falls no lover dies.
    Cease, Celia, cease; restrain thy flowing tears,
Some warmer passion will dispel thy cares.
In man you'll find a more substantial bliss,
More grateful toying, and a sweeter kiss.
    He's dead. Oh lay him gently in the ground!
And may his tomb be by this verse renowned.
Here Shock, the pride of all his kind, is laid;
Who fawned like man, but ne'er like man betrayed.

Sweet William's Farewell to Black-eyed Susan

    All in the Downs the fleet was moored,
        The streamers waving in the wind,
    When black-eyed Susan came aboard.
        Oh! where shall I my true love find!
Tell me, ye jovial sailors, tell me true,
If my sweet William sails among the crew.

    William, who high upon the yard,
        Rocked with the billow to and fro,
    Soon as her well-known voice he heard,
        He sighed, and cast his eyes below:
The cord slides swiftly through his glowing hands,
And, (quick as lightning) on the deck he stands.

    So the sweet lark, high poised in air,
        Shuts close his pinions to his breast,
    (If, chance, his mate's shrill call he hear)
        And drops at once into her nest.
The noblest captain in the British fleet,
Might envy William's lip those kisses sweet.

    O Susan, Susan, lovely dear,
        My vows shall ever true remain;
    Let me kiss off that falling tear,
        We only part to meet again.
Change, as ye list, ye winds; my heart shall be
The faithful compass that still points to thee.

    Believe not what the landmen say,
        Who tempt with doubts thy constant mind:
    They'll tell thee, sailors, when away,
        In ev'ry port a mistress find.
Yes, yes, believe them when they tell thee so,
For thou art present wheresoe'er I go.

    If to far India's coast we sail,
        Thy eyes are seen in di'monds bright,
    Thy breath is Africk's spicy gale,
        Thy skin is ivory, so white.
Thus ev'ry beauteous object that I view,
Wakes in my soul some charm of lovely Sue.

    Though battle call me from thy arms
        Let not my pretty Susan mourn;
    Though canons roar, yet safe from harms,
        William shall to his dear return.
Love turns aside the balls that round me fly,
Lest precious tears should drop from Susan's eye.

    The boatswain gave the dreadful word,
        The sails their swelling bosom spread,
    No longer must she stay aboard:
        They kissed, she sighed, he hung his head.
Her less'ning boat, unwilling rows to land:
Adieu, she cries! and waved her lily hand.

from Trivia; or, the Art of Walking the Streets of London — Book II: Of Walking the Streets By Day

    For ease and for dispatch, the morning's best:
No tides of passengers the street molest.
You'll see a draggled damsel, here and there,
From Billingsgate her fishy traffic bear;
On doors the sallow milk-maid chalks her gains;
Ah! how unlike the milk-maid of the plains!
Before proud gates attending asses bray,
Or arrogate with solemn pace the way;
These grave physicians with their milky cheer,
The love-sick maid and dwindling beau repair;

Here rows of drummers stand in martial file,
And with their vellum thunder shake the pile,
To greet the new-made bride. Are sounds like these
The proper prelude to a state of peace?
Now industry awakes her busy sons,
Full charged with news the breathless hawker runs:
Shops open, coaches roll, carts shake the ground,
And all the streets with passing cries resound.

   If clothed in black, you tread the busy town
Or if distinguished by the rev'rend gown,
Three trades avoid; oft in the mingling press,
The barber's apron soils the sable dress;
Shun the perfumer's touch with cautious eye,
Nor let the baker's step advance too nigh;
Ye walkers too that youthful colours wear,
Three sullying trades avoid with equal care;
The little chimney-sweeper skulks along,
And marks with sooty stains the heedless throng;
When small-coal murmurs in the hoarser throat,
From smutty dangers guard thy threatened coat:
The dust-man's cart offends thy clothes and eyes,
When through the street a cloud of ashes flies;
But whether black or lighter dyes are worn,
The chandler's basket, on his shoulder borne,
With tallow spots thy coat; resign the way,
To shun the surly butcher's greasy tray,
Butcher's, whose hands are dyed with blood's foul stain,
And always foremost in the hangman's train.

   Let due civilities be strictly paid.
The wall surrender to the hooded maid;
Nor let thy sturdy elbow's hasty rage
Jostle the feeble steps of trembling age:
And when the porter bends beneath his load,

And pants for breath, clear thou the crowded road.
But above all, the groping blind direct,
And from the pressing throng the lame protect.
You'll sometimes meet a fop, of nicest tread,
Whose mantling peruke veils his empty head,
At ev'ry step he dreads the wall to lose,
And risks, to save a coach, his red-heeled shoes;
Him, like the miller, pass with caution by,
Lest from his shoulder clouds of powder fly.
But when the bully, with assuming pace,
Cocks his broad hat, edged round with tarnished lace,
Yield not the way; defy his strutting pride,
And thrust him to the muddy kennel's side;
He never turns again, nor dares oppose,
But mutters coward curses as he goes.

[...]

Where famed St. Giles's ancient limits spread,
An inrailed column rears its lofty head,
Here to sev'n streets sev'n dials count the day,
And from each other catch the circling ray.
Here oft the peasant, with enquiring face,
Bewildered, trudges on from place to place;
He dwells on ev'ry sign with stupid gaze,
Enters the narrow alley's doubtful maze,
Tries ev'ry winding court and street in vain,
And doubles o'er his weary steps again.
Thus hardy Theseus with intrepid feet,
Travers'd the dang'rous labyrinth of Crete;
But still the wand'ring passes forced his stay,
Till Ariadne's clue unwinds the way.
But do not thou, like that bold chief, confide
Thy vent'rous footsteps to a female guide;
She'll lead thee with delusive smiles along,
Dive in thy fob, and drop thee in the throng.

Samuel Taylor Coleridge

Coleridge was born in Ottery St Mary in 1772, the youngest son of the vicar. After his father's death Coleridge went to Christ's Hospital School in London, and later studied at Jesus College, Cambridge. It was in Cambridge that he met the radical, and future poet laureate, Robert Southey. He moved with Southey to Bristol to establish a community, but the plan came to nothing. In 1795 he married the sister of Southey's fiancée Sara Fricker, although he was not in love her.

Coleridge's first collection, *Poems On Various Subjects*, was published in 1796, and was followed in 1797 by *Poems*. In 1797 he began the publication of a short-lived liberal political periodical *The Watchman* and then began a close friendship with Dorothy and William Wordsworth, the creative relationship for which they are both famous. From it came *Lyrical Ballads*, which opened with Coleridge's 'Rime of the Ancient Mariner' and ended with Wordsworth's 'Tintern Abbey'. The use of everyday, non-"literary" language and the writers' fresh approach to nature marked a significant break with previous styles.

The Wedgwood brothers granted Coleridge an annuity of £150, enabling him to devote himself to literature. After becoming disenchanted with developments in post-revolutionary France, Coleridge visited Germany in 1798-99 with the Wordsworths, and went on to study philosophy at Göttingen University. In 1809-10, with Sara Hutchinson, he wrote and edited the literary and political magazine *The Friend*. From 1808 to 1818 he gave several lectures, chiefly in London, and gained a reputation as a Shakespearean scholar. In 1810 he fell out with Wordsworth, and the pair's friendship never fully recovered.

Suffering from illnesses throughout his life, Coleridge had become addicted to opium, and he often contemplated suicide, during his later years in London. He had found permanent shelter in Highgate at the home of Dr. James Gillman, and rarely left the house. He was elected a Fellow of the Royal Society of Literature in 1824, and died in Highgate in 1834.

Further reading:
The Complete Poems (ed. Keach, Penguin, London, 1997)

Sonnet: To the River Otter

Dear native brook! wild streamlet of the west!
   How many various-fated years have past,
   What happy and what mournful hours, since last
I skimmed the smooth thin stone along thy breast,
Numbering its light leaps! yet so deep impressed
Sink the sweet scenes of childhood, that mine eyes
   I never shut amid the sunny ray,
But straight with all their tints thy waters rise,
   Thy crossing plank, thy marge with willows grey,
And bedded sand that veined with various dyes
Gleamed through thy bright transparence! On my way,
   Visions of childhood! oft have ye beguiled
Lone manhood's cares, yet waking fondest sighs:
   Ah! that once more I were a careless child!

Kubla Khan

In Xanadu did Kubla Khan
A stately pleasure-dome decree:
Where Alph, the sacred river, ran
Through caverns measureless to man
Down to a sunless sea.
So twice five miles of fertile ground
With walls and towers were girdled round:
And there were gardens bright with sinuous rills,
Where blossomed many an incense-bearing tree;
And here were forests ancient as the hills,
Enfolding sunny spots of greenery.
But oh! that deep romantic chasm which slanted
Down the green hill athwart a cedarn cover!
A savage place! as holy and enchanted
As e'er beneath a waning moon was haunted

By woman wailing for her demon-lover!
And from this chasm, with ceaseless turmoil seething,
As if this earth in fast thick pants were breathing,
A mighty fountain momently was forced:
Amid whose swift half-intermitted burst
Huge fragments vaulted like rebounding hail,
Or chaffy grain beneath the thresher's flail:
And 'mid these dancing rocks at once and ever
It flung up momently the sacred river.
Five miles meandering with a mazy motion
Through wood and dale the sacred river ran,
Then reached the caverns measureless to man,
And sank in tumult to a lifeless ocean:
And 'mid this tumult Kubla heard from far
Ancestral voices prophesying war!

The shadow of the dome of pleasure
Floated midway on the waves;
Where was heard the mingled measure
From the fountain and the caves.
It was a miracle of rare device,
A sunny pleasure-dome with caves of ice!
A damsel with a dulcimer
In a vision once I saw:
It was an Abyssinian maid,
And on her dulcimer she played,
Singing of Mount Abora.
Could I revive within me
Her symphony and song,
To such a deep delight 'twould win me,
That with music loud and long,
I would build that dome in air,
That sunny dome! those caves of ice!
And all who heard should see them there,
And all should cry, Beware! Beware!

His flashing eyes, his floating hair!
Weave a circle round him thrice,
And close your eyes with holy dread,
For he on honey-dew hath fed,
And drunk the milk of Paradise.

The Nightingale – *A Conversation Poem. April, 1798*

No cloud, no relic of the sunken day
Distinguishes the West, no long thin slip
Of sullen light, no obscure trembling hues
Come, we will rest on this old mossy bridge!
You see the glimmer of the stream beneath,
But hear no murmuring: it flows silently,
O'er its soft bed of verdure. All is still,
A balmy night! and though the stars be dim,
Yet let us think upon the vernal showers
That gladden the green earth, and we shall find
A pleasure in the dimness of the stars.
And hark! the nightingale begins its song
"Most musical, most melancholy" bird!
A melancholy bird! Oh! idle thought!
In nature there is nothing melancholy.
But some night-wandering man whose heart was pierced
With the remembrance of a grievous wrong,
Or slow distemper, or neglected love,
  (And so, poor wretch! filled all things with himself,
And made all gentle sounds tell back the tale
Of his own sorrow) he, and such as he,
First named these notes a melancholy strain.
And many a poet echoes the conceit;
Poet who hath been building up the rhyme
When he had better far have stretched his limbs

Beside a brook in mossy forest-dell,
By sun or moon-light, to the influxes
Of shapes and sounds and shifting elements
Surrendering his whole spirit, of his song
And of his fame forgetful! so his fame
Should share in nature's immortality,
A venerable thing! and so his song
Should make all nature lovelier, and itself
Be loved like nature! But 'twill not be so;
And youths and maidens most poetical,
Who lose the deepening twilights of the spring
In ball-rooms and hot theatres, they still
Full of meek sympathy must heave their sighs
O'er Philomela's pity-pleading strains.

My friend, and thou, our sister! we have learnt
A different lore; we may not thus profane
Nature's sweet voices, always full of love
And joyance! 'Tis the merry nightingale
That crowds, and hurries, and precipitates
With fast thick warble his delicious notes,
As he were fearful that an April night
Would be too short for him to utter forth
His love-chant, and disburthen his full soul
Of all its music!

And I know a grove
Of large extent, hard by a castle huge,
Which the great lord inhabits not; and so
This grove is wild with tangling underwood,
And the trim walks are broken up, and grass,
Thin grass and king-cups grow within the paths.
But never elsewhere in one place I knew
So many nightingales; and far and near,
In wood and thicket, over the wide grove,

They answer and provoke each other's song,
With skirmish and capricious passagings,
And murmurs musical and swift jug jug,
And one low piping sound more sweet than all—
Stirring the air with such a harmony,
That should you close your eyes, you might almost
Forget it was not day! On moon-lit bushes,
Whose dewy leaflets are but half disclosed,
You may perchance behold them on the twigs,
Their bright, bright eyes, their eyes both bright and full,
Glistening, while many a glow-worm in the shade
Lights up her love-torch.

A most gentle maid,
Who dwelleth in her hospitable home
Hard by the castle, and at latest eve
(Even like a lady vowed and dedicate
To something more than nature in the grove)
Glides through the pathways; she knows all their notes,
That gentle maid! and oft, a moment's space,
What time the moon was lost behind a cloud,
Hath heard a pause of silence; till the moon
Emerging, hath awakened earth and sky
With one sensation, and these wakeful birds
Have all burst forth in choral minstrelsy,
As if some sudden gale had swept at once
A hundred airy harps! And she hath watched
Many a nightingale perched giddily
On blossomy twig still swinging from the breeze,
And to that motion tune his wanton song
Like tipsy joy that reels with tossing head.

Farewell, O warbler! till to-morrow eve,
And you, my friends! farewell, a short farewell!
We have been loitering long and pleasantly,

And now for our dear homes.—That strain again!
Full fain it would delay me! My dear babe,
Who, capable of no articulate sound,
Mars all things with his imitative lisp,
How he would place his hand beside his ear,
His little hand, the small forefinger up,
And bid us listen! And I deem it wise
To make him Nature's play-mate. He knows well
The evening-star! and once, when he awoke
In most distressful mood (some inward pain
Had made up that strange thing, an infant's dream—)
I hurried with him to our orchard-plot,
And he beheld the moon, and, hushed at once,
Suspends his sobs, and laughs most silently,
While his fair eyes, that swam with undropped tears,
Did glitter in the yellow moon-beam! Well!—
It is a father's tale: But if that Heaven
Should give me life, his childhood shall grow up
Familiar with these songs, that with the night
He may associate joy.—Once more, farewell,
Sweet nightingale! Once more, my friends! farewell.

Lines on a Friend, Who Died of a Frenzy Fever, Induced by Calumnious Reports

Edmund! thy grave with aching eye I scan,
And inly groan for heaven's poor outcast, man!
'Tis tempest all or gloom: in early youth,
If gifted with the Ithuriel lance of truth,
We force to start amid her feigned caress
Vice, siren-hag! in native ugliness,
A brother's fate will haply rouse the tear:
Onward we move in heaviness and fear!
But if our fond hearts call to pleasure's bower

Some pigmy folly in a careless hour,
The faithless guest shall stamp th' enchanted ground
And mingled forms of mis'ry rise around:
Heart-fretting fear, with pallid look aghast,
That courts the future woe to hide the past;
Remorse, the poisoned arrow in his side;
And loud lewd mirth, to anguish close allied:
Till frenzy, fierce-eyed child of moping pain,
Darts her hot lightning flash athwart the brain.

Rest, injured shade! Shall slander squatting near
Spit her cold venom in a dead man's ear?
'Twas thine to feel the sympathetic glow
In merit's joy, and poverty's meek woe;
Thine all, that cheer the moment as it flies,
The zoneless cares, and smiling courtesies.
Nursed in thy heart the firmer virtues grew,
And in thy heart they withered! Such chill dew
Wan indolence on each young blossom shed;
And vanity her filmy net-work spread,
With eye that rolled around in asking gaze,
And tongue that trafficked in the trade of praise.
Thy follies such! the hard world marked them well –
Were they more wise, the proud who never fell?

Rest, injured shade! the poor man's grateful prayer
On heaven-ward wing thy wounded soul shall bear.
As oft at twilight gloom thy grave I pass,
And oft sit down upon its recent grass,
With introverted eye I contemplate
Similitude of soul, perhaps of—fate!

To me hath Heaven with bounteous hand assigned
Energetic reason and a shaping mind,
The daring ken of truth, the patriot's part,

And pity's sigh, that breathes the gentle heart—
Sloth-jaundiced all! and from my graspless hand
Drop friendship's precious pearls, like hour-glass sand.
I weep, yet stoop not! the faint anguish flows,
A dreamy pang in the morning's fev'rish doze.

Is this piled earth our being's passless mound?
Tell me, cold grave! is death with poppies crowned?
Tired sentinel! mid fitful starts I nod,
And fain would sleep, though pillowed on a clod!

To the Reverend George Coleridge, of Ottery St. Mary, Devon

A blessed lot hath he, who having past
His youth and early manhood in the stir
And turmoil of the world, retreats at length,
With cares that move, not agitate the heart,
To the same dwelling where his father dwelt;
And haply views his tottering little ones
Embrace those aged knees, and climb that lap,
On which first kneeling his own infancy
Lisped its brief prayer. Such, O my earliest friend!
Thine and thy brothers' favourable lot.
At distance did ye climb life's upland road,
Yet cheered and cheering: now fraternal love
Hath drawn you to one centre. Be your days
Holy, and blest and blessing may ye live!

To me th' Eternal Wisdom hath dispensed
A different fortune and more different mind –
Me from the spot where first I sprang to light,
Too soon transplanted, ere my soul had fixed

Its first domestic loves; and hence through life
Chasing chance-started friendships. A brief while
Some have preserved me from life's pelting ills;
But, like a tree with leaves of feeble stem,
If the clouds lasted, or a sudden breeze
Ruffled the boughs, they on my head at once
Dropped the collected shower: and some most false,
False and fair-foliaged as the manchineel,
Have tempted me to slumber in their shade
E'en mid the storm; then breathing subtlest damps,
Mixed their own venom with the rain from heaven,
That I woke poisoned! But (the praise be His
Who gives us all things) more have yielded me
Permanent shelter: and beside one friend,
I, as beneath the covert of an oak,
Have raised a lowly shed, and know the names
Of husband and of father; nor unhearing
Of that divine and nightly-whispering voice,
Which from my childhood to maturer years
Spake to me of predestinated wreaths,
Bright with no fading colours!
    Yet at times
My soul is sad, that I have roamed through life
Still most a stranger, most with naked heart,
At mine own home and birth-place: chiefly then,
When I remember thee, my earliest friend!
Thee, who didst watch my boyhood and my youth;
Didst trace my wanderings with a father's eye;
And, boding evil yet still hoping good,
Rebuked each fault and wept o'er all my woes.
Who counts the beatings of the lonely heart,
That Being knows, how I have loved thee ever,
Loved as a brother, as a son revered thee!
O 'tis to me an ever new delight,
To talk of thee and thine; or when the blast

Of the shrill winter, rattling our rude sash,
Endears the cleanly hearth and social bowl;
Or when, as now, on some delicious eve,
We in our sweet sequestered orchard-plot
Sit on the tree crooked earthward; whose old boughs,
That hand above us in an arborous roof,
Stirred by the faint gale of departing May,
Send their loose blossoms slanting o'er our heads!

Nor dost thou sometimes recall those hours,
When with the joy of hope thou gav'st thine ear
To my wild firstling lays. Since then my song
Hath sounded deeper notes, such as beseem
Of that sad wisdom, folly leaves behind;
Or the high raptures of prophetic faith;
Or such as, tuned to these tumultuous times,
Cope with the tempest's swell!
     These various songs,
Which I have framed in many a various mood,
Accept, my brother; and (for some perchance
Will strike discordant on thy milder mind)
If aught of error or intemperate truth
Should meet thine ear, think thou that riper age
Will calm it down, and let thy loves forgive it!

www.ingramcontent.com/pod-product-compliance
Lightning Source LLC
Chambersburg PA
CBHW031152160426
43193CB00008B/338